KNITTING 1920's AND 30's

Originals

Nancy Vale

Mills & Boon Limited,
London, Sydney, Toronto

First published in Great Britain 1979 by Mills & Boon
Limited, 17–19 Foley Street, London WIA IDR

© Nancy Vale

ISBN 0 263 (cased) 06414 x
          (limp) 06420 4

Printed in Great Britain by
Fletcher & Son Ltd, Norwich

Design, layout and original artwork:
Mushroom Production · London

CONTENTS

The charm of the 1920s and 30s

I find it most exciting to publish my first book of patterns based on styles with the look of the 1920–40 period. Hand-knitted clothes from that era hold for me a very special appeal and charm. During this time knitting fashions changed from the long, loose, figure-hiding look of the early twenties to the short, figure-hugging, puffed-sleeve look of the late thirties. Between them they embrace some of the most charming knitted garments of all time – and with the superb choice of yarns and colours available today, these delectable gems of the past can re-emerge as all-time classics. With the introduction of thicker yarns they can also now be made much more quickly.

Colour too reflects the changing 'moods' of fashion. In the early 1920s colour inclined towards pale pastels reflecting the somewhat demure, chaste look. Gradually warmer pastels took over, with touches of bright rich colours – these becoming increasingly popular in the late 1930s. For some years now, natural earthy colours have remained the popular basics around which come and go colours of every hue – from the lovely very subtle new shades to the exciting rich tones. To me colour is a very important part of design. I love colour and there are endless enchanting blends that can do so much for a garment and give so much pleasure to the knitter. I have given a few colour suggestions in some of the patterns, but never be afraid to try a new colour or mix what may seem unusual – the end product can be delightful!

On page 16 I mention brief and simple adjustments that can be made to basic styles to meet changing fashion.

Although I have mainly concentrated on a variety of women's styles in this book, the men are not forgotten and you will find a number of styles which are suitable for both sexes.

I hope this book will be your constant knitting companion and the garments made from it a treasured part of your wardrobe.

2 COLOUR PATT
JACKET IM
DK.

GENERAL NOTES

The patterns in this book are made mostly in double-knitting or 4-ply yarn. Particular brands have not been specified because there is no reason why knitters should not use their own favourite brands, or one of those most easily available to them. The need for a subtle matching colour will also sometimes dictate a particular brand. In fact, the brand used makes very little difference to the resultant garment – as long as a double-knitting yarn is used for a double-knitting pattern, a 4-ply for a 4-ply pattern and so on. Crepe twist wool and even some speciality yarns such as bouclé of equivalent thickness may also be used.

The all-important factor is to get your tension right against the pattern (and different knitters produce quite incredible differences in tension). It is a simple question of adjusting needle size to achieve the tension specified. You should always knit a sample square of at least 10 cm (4 in) and check its size for the number of stitches given in the tension note at the beginning of each pattern. If your knitted sample measurement is larger than that specified your tension is too loose, so try a smaller needle. If your knitted sample measurement is smaller your tension is too tight, so try a larger needle. Then change all your needles correspondingly up or down throughout a pattern.

I usually use pure wool for my garments – for practical reasons as well as comfort and the obvious appeal of its appearance. Wool knits up beautifully, is excellent for keeping shape (giving good elasticity to welts, etc.) and washes admirably. It makes little difference if there is a small percentage of nylon, acrylic or mohair included in the yarn.

Hand knitting

Many knitters like myself have been tempted at some time to try a knitting machine, but have found that the resultant garment looks different, feels different and seems to absorb more yarn. Although sophisticated machines have a very real place in the modern world they cannot take the place of hand knitting which is indeed becoming increasingly popular all over the world. It is an extraordinarily therapeutic and relaxing pastime which can be done almost anywhere, at any time, while being tremendously satisfying and rewarding.

Some knitting terms

Casting off Patterns specify whether this should be done *knitwise* (usual way) or *ribwise*. If ribwise, the needle should be put to front and back of stitches alternately as if knitting rib. In this way the necessary elasticity will be maintained at the edge of the garment.
Flatstitch To achieve a neat seam, place the two knitted pieces of the garment together and oversew between the two notched edges (see note on page 15) to join.
Garter stitch Knit every stitch of every row.

YOUNG LADY'S DIARY

1939

"And don't forget," I said, "they are 'men' at the 'Varsity, not 'boys'; and Courts are Quads at Oxford; and. . . ." Mary squeezed my arm.

"Isn't it thrilling, Anne?" she said.

"Your first visit to Oxford, and my first trip since I 'ran-in' my Ford V-8. I'm thrilled, too. I can step on it at last!"

"It's a dream, Anne . . . I mean the car." That's what I was thinking.

My father winced when I suggested a Ford V-8. He thought that a luxury eight-cylindered car would be beyond his means. But I told him how little extra it cost to step up into the V-8 class, and several V-8 owners proved how low running expenses were. (Actually, I've been getting between 22 and 27 miles to the gallon.) So father gave in. He's as excited as I am now.

"Seventy up this hill is pretty marvellous," said Mary, "and it doesn't feel as though we're doing more than fifty."

It was that long gradient just beyond High Wycombe, the one that shows up so many cars. I can honestly say that the V-8 didn't notice it. Never had I known that driving a motor car could be so thrilling. Nor so easy, because I felt quite safe at speed, although I'm not a so-called expert driver.

* * *

We reached Oxford in an hour and a half and went straight to the rooms that Peter and John share. Mary was twittering.

"Don't *seem* so excited," I had said, but without effect.

"We didn't expect you for half-an-hour," said Peter; "you must have travelled, Anne."

"It's her new car," said Mary; "she passed everything with the greatest of ease. What a lovely Court you live in, John!"

"Nice, isn't it?" said John; "funny, but we call them Quads at Oxford. What kind of car?"

"Oh, I *am* sorry! I forgot." She blushed furiously. "A Ford V-8 . . . a new one, just run in."

"No wonder you're early! There are very few cars that can compete with a Ford V-8, regardless of cost. Nothing to touch them for value and they're darn fine engineering jobs. I'd give my eye-teeth for one." This, from mechanically-minded John, was praise indeed. I smiled.

"Any Ford owner will tell you that, John."

* * *

It was a perfect day. We drove the boys (men, I mean) round to the Mitre for lunch. It was warm enough for the river, and we ended up with tea in their rooms.

"I wish we could drive back with you," said Peter as we got ready to go. "I'd love to drive that car of yours."

"We hope to bring up a 'Prefect' next term," said John. "That's the next best thing to a V-8. Sports performance at a price we paupers can afford."

As they saw us off, Peter drew Mary aside. "Oh, and Mary," I heard him say, "about the Eights Week Ball. I was wondering if you . . ."

FORD V-8 Saloon de Luxe £280, Convertible Coupé £300; the 'Prefect', the Ten ahead of its class, Saloon £145, Double-Entrance Saloon £152. 10., Touring Car £155; prices at Works.

Moss stitch Knit one stitch, purl one stitch all along the row. Next row turn but repeat first row exactly so that now a knit stitch matches a purl stitch and vice versa (as opposed to rib where knit stitch matches knit and purl stitch matches purl).

Stocking stitch Alternately knit one row and purl the next.

Two very important tips
Whenever possible as you knit, slip the first stitch and knit into the back of the last stitch on *every* row. This gives neat, tidy edges, where edges show, and also makes little notches along the edges enabling you to sew up easily and neatly by just flatstitching or oversewing the notches together. It also makes it easier to align piece to piece (see note on flatstitch page 12). Never join yarn in the middle of a row. If you feel that the yarn will run out before you finish the row, leave the excess hanging at the beginning of the row for sewing up and start a new ball.

Measurements
Metric measurements are given throughout the book with the imperial equivalents in inches, ounces, etc. in brackets. The following list of corresponding measurements may serve as a handy reference guide.

Bust/chest sizes in metric and Imperial measurements

cm	81	86	91	97	102	107
in	32	34	36	38	40	42

Metric needle sizes are also used, with the old English equivalent in brackets, at the start of each pattern. The following chart gives these equivalents and also lists corresponding American needle sizes.

Knitting needle sizes

ENGLISH SIZE	METRIC	AMERICAN
000	9	15
00	$8\frac{1}{2}$	13
0	8	12
1	$7\frac{1}{2}$	11
2	7	$10\frac{1}{2}$
3	$6\frac{1}{2}$	10
4	6	9
5	$5\frac{1}{2}$	8
6	5	7
7	$4\frac{1}{2}$	6
8	4	5
9	$3\frac{1}{2}$	4
10	$3\frac{1}{4}$	3
11	3	2
12	$2\frac{1}{2}$	1
13	$2\frac{1}{4}$	0
14	2	00

Stitch-Holders
A stitch-holder, spare needle or large safety-pin may be used where it is necessary to leave a number of stitches aside before picking up later (as for a neckband).

Abbreviations

alt.	: alternate
beg.	: beginning
c	: cable
dec.	: decrease
inc.	: increase
k	: knit
m	: make
mb	: make bobble (woolly ball)
mk	: make knot
p	: purl
psso	: pass slip stitch over
rep.	: repeat
sl	: slip
st	: stitch
tbl	: through back of loop
tog.	: together
wl.fwd	: wool forward
wrn	: wool round needle
yrn	: yarn round needle

Note
Fair Isle charts have been included for the sleeveless Jacquard cardigan and the old-fashioned 4-ply cardigan. Where brief instructions for a patterned yoke only have been required (as in the case of the double-knit cardigan with Jacquard yoke), these have simply been incorporated into the general text.

Washing

I would always advise hand washing garments with wool or mohair content. Man-made fibres can of course be machine washed. Today washing instructions will usually be found on yarn wrappers. Hand-knitted garments, if washed correctly, will give years of wear. Hand wash in *warm* water. Rinse *well* and after rinsing fold the garment carefully, giving it a *very short* spin to take the water weight out of the garment. Refold, hand smoothing while folding into shape – then the garment can be hung out to dry or gently tumble dried. Tumble drying on a *low* heat keeps woollen garments beautifully soft. Anyway, this is the way I wash my woollens week after week and they all keep perfect shape. I have even done my mohair sweater the same way.

Pressing

The entire finish of a woollen garment is improved with pressing. It is usually best to join up the shoulder seams and neatly sew sleeves into armholes – if there are sleeves – and then press garment still open with a warm iron and damp cloth. Mohair, in my opinion, should never be pressed. I find it perfectly adequate to smooth and fold with the hands. Similarly, I do not advise pressing coarse or heavy texture stitches.

As far as acrylic yarns are concerned, do be very careful about pressing. All too easily pressing can knock all life out of a yarn, making the garment go limp and shapeless. I never press acrylics; I just smooth the garment into shape with my hands and fold it very carefully. However, with so many speciality yarns available these days I would advise careful reading of instructions on the yarn label.

Adjustments

Very simple adjustments to these patterns can be successfully achieved – even by inexperienced knitters – giving the garment a totally different look and purpose. Necklines can be made round, square, straight (boat neck) or 'V' shaped. Collars may be added or omitted, sleeves can be made long or short, tailored, puffed or dropped. A sleeved garment can be made sleeveless, pockets may be added or removed. Cardigans can be made 'V' necked, or open to the neck. Length can of course be changed and a garment can be made larger and looser by using a larger needle (normally about one needle size bigger will make a garment one size larger).

Varied use of colour is another effective way of ringing the changes. A garment in fancy stitch could be made in stocking stitch in a lovely blend of stripes, or with a band of stripes here and there. A band of Fair Isle or Jacquard could be added above the welt or on the yoke (or on both) and immediately above the sleeve welt. Colour may also be introduced with simple embroidery. Moreover, you can use clusters of beads or sequins to change a day sweater or cardigan into a delightful one for the evening.

A totally different look can be achieved by making a garment in an alternative yarn. There are a wide variety of yarns available. Fancy speciality yarns rarely need stitch detail, for example bouclé yarns look beautiful in reverse stocking stitch. But it must be remembered that when substituting one finish of yarn for another it is most important to test tension by knitting a sample tension square.

Lastly, different stitches offer variety. When a different stitch is used care should be taken to see that the number of stitches required for the pattern fit into the number cast on. One or two more or less will make little or no difference to the size of the finished garment. There are some lacy stitches that include increasing and decreasing as part of the pattern and these can cause problems where shaping is required. With such stitches a charming effect is achieved by using the fancy stitch up to the armhole, then doing whole yoke and sleeves simply, say in moss stitch.

KNITTING

Long, loose tube sweater

Measurements (To be worn loose) Bust: 92 [102] cm (36 [40] in). Sleeve seam: 46 [48] cm (18 [19] in)

Materials 15 [16] × 25 gm balls of mohair yarn

Needles A pair each of 3¼-mm (No. 10), 4-mm (No. 8) and 6½-mm (No. 3)

Abbreviations See page 16

Tension 7 sts equal 5 cm (2 in) using 6½-mm needles

Back With 4-mm needles cast on 63 sts [69 sts], work in single rib for 8 cm (3 in). Change to 6½-mm needles and work in stocking st till work is 46 cm (18 in). Mark this row with a piece of coloured thread to show start of armhole and then continue in stocking st till work measures 71 cm (28 in) from start, finishing at end of a knit row. **Cast off knitwise.**

Front Work as for back till work measures 46 cms (18 in) ending at end of a purl row. **Start 'V' neck shaping** as follows: k31 [34], turn, leaving remaining stitches on a spare needle. **Next row:** k2 tog tbl, purl to end. Work in stocking st for 3 rows. Repeat last 4 rows until 22 stitches remain. Continue straight till front measures same as back. **Cast off** knitwise on wrong side. Rejoin yarn to remaining stitches, leaving centre stitch on a safety-pin to pick up for neckband, work across the remaining 31 sts [34 sts]. Then work this side to match first side.

Sleeves (2)
Using 3¼-mm needles cast on 42 sts and work in single rib for 10 cm (4in) increasing in every other stitch on last row

(63 sts). Change to 6½-mm needles and work in stocking st until sleeve measures 46 [48] cm (18 [19] in). **Cast off** *loosely*

Neckband
Sew up right shoulder seam, then with right side of work facing and using 3¼-mm needles pick up and knit 65 sts down left front neck, the centre 'V' st from safety-pin (marking this stitch with a coloured thread), 65 sts up other front neck and 20 sts across back neck (151 sts). Work in single rib *dec. 1 stitch* either side of centre stitch on every row, working 8 rows in all (135 sts). **Cast off** *ribwise.*

Making up
Sew up rest of seams neatly making sure sleeve lies evenly and flat.

18

KNITTING

Cloche hat and scarf

With her sweater the girl of the early 1920s often wore a close-fitting cloche hat

Cloche hat (using mohair yarn double)

Measurements This little cloche, being made in double yarn, fits all normal sizes
Materials 4 × 25 gm balls of mohair yarn
Needles 1 pair of 5-mm (No. 6)
Abbreviations See page 16
Method
Using 5-mm needles and double yarn cast on 82 sts and work in single rib for 15 cm (6 in). Shape crown as follows, working in garter st.
1st row: *k6, k2 tog., rep. from * to last 2 sts, k2.
2nd and alternate rows: knit
3rd row: *k5, k2 tog., rep. from * to last 2 sts, k2.
5th row: *k4, k2 tog., rep. from * to last 2 sts, k2.
7th row: *k3, k2 tog., rep. from * to last 2 sts, k2.
9th row: *k2, k2 tog., rep. from * to last 2 sts, k2.
11th row: *k1, k2 tog., rep. from * to last 2 sts, k2.
12th row: *k2 tog., all along the row then draw yarn through stitches.

Making up
Sew up back seam.

Scarf

Materials 6 × 25 gm balls of mohair yarn and 1 pair of 5½-mm (No. 5) needles
Method
Using mohair yarn single and 5½-mm (No. 5) needles cast on 36 sts and work in single rib for 183 cm (72 in). **Cast off ribwise.**
Fringe
Cut strands of mohair yarn 36 cm (14 in) long and fringe 5 strands together 13 times along cast-on and cast-off edges of scarf.

Knit Yourself This NEW TUNIC SUIT

TUNIC suits are new, smart and flattering. If you want to be right in the mode, seize your knitting-needles now and make sure of chic!

ISN'T this stitch a fascinating one? You'd like the tunic in dark marsh brown, with the smart slim skirt and those effective buttons in pewter grey.

Materials Required

Faudel's A.A. Peacock Quality Fingering 4-fold 1 lb. in main colour; 8 oz. in a contrasting colour.

Double Century knitting pins, two No. 9; two No. 10; two No. 7.

16 buttons.

¾ yard material for skirt top.

Measurements

The Tunic.—Shoulder to lower edge, 38 inches; round tunic below armholes, when fastened, 37 inches; sleeve seam, 19 inches.

Always knit into back of each cast-on stitch.

Abbreviations.—K., knit; p., purl; inc., increase; dec., decrease; st., stitch; sts., stitches; beg., beginning; pat., pattern; m., make (by bringing wool forward between needles and over right-hand needle).

THE TUNIC

The Back.—Cast on with main colour wool and No. 9 pins, 141 sts. Work in moss-stitch as follows : **1st row**—* K. 1, p. 1, repeat from * to end of row, end k. 1. Continue this row for 2 inches. Cast on 1 st. at beg. of next row. Then work in pat. as follows : **1st row**—* K. 4, p. 2, repeat from * to last 4 sts.; k. 4. **2nd row**—* P. 4, k. 2, repeat from * to last 4 sts. p. 4. **3rd row**—Purl. **4th row**—Knit. **5th row**—As 2nd. **6th row**—As 1st. Repeat 5th and 6th rows once more. **9th row**—Purl. **10th row**—Knit. These 10 rows form one pattern. Repeat these 10 rows once more (20 rows altogether). Now dec. 1 st. each end of next row, then every first pat. row following until 116 sts. (a dec.

of 26 sts.). Continue in pat. until work measures 22 inches from start. Change to No. 10 pins and work for 3 inches. Change to No. 9 pins and work for 6 inches. Shape armholes. Cast off 4 sts. at beg. of the next 6 rows (a dec. of 12 sts. each side). Continue until armholes measure 7 inches. Shape shoulders. Cast off 8 sts. at the beg. of the next 8 rows (32 sts. for each shoulder). Cast off the 28 sts. left for the back of the neck.

Front (Left when worn).—Cast on 81 sts. with main colour wool and No. 9 pins. Work in moss-stitch for 2 inches. (Cast on 1 st. 82 sts.) Change to pat. as for the back. But keep 12 sts. in moss-stitch at the front edge for border. When you have worked 20 rows of pat. dec. one st. at beg. of the next row (underarm side) and then every 10th row following until 72 sts. (a dec. of 10 sts.). Continue until work measures 22 inches. Change to No. 10 pins, work for 3 inches. Change to No. 9 pins, work for 6 inches. Shape armhole. Cast off 4 sts. at the beg. of the next 3 armhole end rows (a dec. of 12 sts.). Continue on the remaining 60 sts. until armhole measures 6 inches. Shape neck. Cast off 28 sts. at neck edge. Continue on the remaining 32 sts. for one inch. Shape shoulder. Cast off 8 sts. at beg. of every armhole end row until all are cast off.

The Right Front.—Make as for left front with dec. and border of 12 sts. on other side. and make buttonholes in border starting the first after one inch of moss-stitch, and then on every 20th row following. Make buttonhole thus : moss-stitch 3, cast off 4, moss-stitch to end of row. **Next row**—Moss-stitch back, cast on 4 sts. moss-stitch 3. Then on the next 20th following row, moss-stitch 3, cast off 4, moss-stitch 5, pat. to end of row. **Next row**—Pat. back, moss-stitch 5, cast on 4, moss-stitch 3. Make 16 button-holes in all.

The Sleeves (both alike).—Cast on with main colour wool and No. 10 pins 60 sts. Rib in k. 1, p. 1, for 3 inches. Change to No. 9 pins and work in pattern 10 rows. Then inc. on the first pat. row and afterwards every first pat. row until 84 sts. When sleeve measures 20 ins. from start, cast off 4 sts. at beg. of next 2 rows and afterwards cast off 2 sts. at beg. of every row until 16 sts. left. Cast off.

The Tie.—Cast on with main colour and No. 7 pins 33 sts. Work in pat. * k. 1, m. 1, k. 2, tog., repeat from * all along row. Work for 10 rows. Dec. 1 st. each end of next and every 8th row until 21 sts. Work for 2 inches, then inc. 1 st. each end of every 8th row until 33 sts. Work for 10 rows. Cast off.

Slots for Tie.—With main colour wool and No. 9 pins, cast on 13 sts. Work in moss-stitch, then dec. 1 st. each end of every other row until 2 sts. Cast off.

THE SKIRT

With contrasting colour wool and No. 9 pins cast on 180 sts.

1st row—K. 4, p. 1, all along row.

2nd row—Purl. Repeat these 2 rows for 15 inches. Cast off. Work another piece in same way.

TO MAKE UP

The Tunic.—Sew up shoulder seams, sew up side seams, sew up sleeve seams, sew in sleeves. Work buttonholes. Sew on slots at neck, one at back and one at each side of front. Thread tie through slots round neck. Press well with warm iron and damp cloth. Sew on buttons.

The Skirt.—Press the skirt carefully with a warm iron and a damp cloth. Sew up the side seams. Make a skirt top of material and sew it neatly to top of knitted skirt.

KNITTING

Sleeveless basket stitch slipover

Measurements (Worn very loose on ladies) Bust: 102 [107, 112] cm (40 [42, 44] in). Length: 69 [69, 71] cm (27 [27, 28] in)

Materials 15 × 25 gm balls of double-knitting yarn

Needles A pair each of 3¼-mm (No. 10) and 5-mm (No. 6)

Abbreviations See page 16

Tension 15 sts and 20 rows equal a pattern square of 8 cm (3 in) using 5-mm needles

Front

Using 3¼-mm needles cast on 98 [106, 114] sts and work in single rib for 9 cm (3½ in). Change to 5-mm needles and basket st pattern as follows: **1st row**: sl1, *k4, p4, rep. from * to last st, knit into the back of this last st. Rep. this row 3 times more. **5th row**: sl1, *p4, k4, rep. from * to last st, knit into the back of this last st. Rep. this row 3 times more. These 8 rows form the pattern which is to be used throughout the garment other than for welts, armbands and neckband. Continue working straight in basket st until work measures 42 cm (16½ in). **Shape armhole**: by casting off 6 sts at the beg. of the next 2 rows. Continue to work straight until work measures 48 cm (19 in) **Shape: 'V' neck**: working across 43 [47, 51] sts, turn. **Next row**: sl1, work 2 sts tog., work to end, knitting into back of last st. Work 3 rows without shaping. Rep. last 4 rows until 33 [36, 39] sts remain, then continue straight until work measures 69 [69, 71] cm (27 [27, 28] in) from beg.,

finishing at the armhole edge. **Shape shoulders**: by casting off 11 [12, 13] sts at the beg. of the next and following 2 alt. rows. Work other side the same reversing, all shapings.

Back

Work exactly as for front up to armhole shaping. **Shape armholes**: by casting off 6 sts at beg. of next 2 rows and then continue working straight until work measures same as front up to shoulders. Cast off 11 [12, 13] sts at the beg. of the next 6 rows – leave remaining sts on spare needle to pick up for neckband.

Neckband

Using 3¼-mm needles and right side facing, pick up 64 sts down left front of 'V', 1st from the centre (marking this st with a piece of coloured yarn), 64 sts from other side of 'V' and then the sts from the centre back. Work 7 rows in single rib working 2 st tog. on either side of centre st (marked with coloured yarn) on *every* row. **Cast off** loosely in rib. The best way is to have a 5-mm needle in your right hand whilst casting off.

Armbands (2)

Sew up shoulder seams and then using 3¼-mm needles and right side of work facing – starting from the start of the straight part of the armhole (the 6 cast-off sts will be sewn to the depth of the rib band you are working) – pick up 144 sts evenly round armhole. Work 6 rows in single rib. **Cast off** loosely in rib.

Making up

Sew depth of armband rib to 6 cast-off sts of armhole. Sew up side seams of garment.

KNITTING

Diamond stitch cardigan

Measurements Worn loosely, as it should be, the first size will fit sizes up to 91 cm (36 in) and second size all larger sizes. Sleeve seams can be made longer or shorter.
Materials 24 × 25 gm balls of double-knitting yarn, 6 buttons to match
Needles A pair each of 3½-mm (No. 9) and 4½-mm (No. 7)
Abbreviations See page 16
Tension 11sts equal 5 cm (2 in) using 4½-mm needles

Back
With 3½-mm needles and double-knitting yarn cast on 98 [110] sts and work in single rib for 9 cm (3½ in). Change to 4½-mm needles and diamond pattern as follows: **1st row**: sl1, k3 *p1, k5, rep. from * to last 4 sts, p1, k2, k1 tbl. **2nd row**: sl1, p1, *k1, p1, k1, p3, rep. from * to last 6 sts, k1, p1, k1, p2, k1 tbl. **3rd row**: sl1, *k1, p1, k3, p1. rep. from * to last st, k1 tbl. **4th row**: sl1, *p5, k1, rep. from * to last st, k1 tbl. **5th row**: as 3rd. **6th row**: as 2nd. **7th row**: as 1st. **8th row**: as 2nd. **9th row**: as 3rd. **10th row**: as 4th. **11th row**: as 3rd. **12th row**: as 2nd. These 12 rows complete the pattern which is used throughout the garment other than for welts and neckband. Continue working straight until work measures 69 [71] cm (27 [28] in) ending at armhole edge. **Shape shoulders:** by casting off 11 [12] sts at beg. of next 6 rows. **Cast off** remaining sts.

Fronts (2)
Cast on 44 [50] sts and work in single rib for 9 cm (3½ in). Change to 4½-mm needles and work in pattern as for back until work is 42 [45] cm (16½ [17½] in) from beg. ending at front edge. **Start shaping 'V' neck slope in next row:** sl1, work 2 sts tog. and being very careful to keep pattern correct, work to end. Work 3 rows without shaping. Repeat last 4 rows until 33 [36] sts remain, then continue to work straight until work is 69 [71] cm (27 [28] in) ending at armhole edge. **Shape shoulders:** by casting off 11 [12] sts at beg. of next and following 2 alt. rows. Work other front exactly the same way, reversing all shapings.

Sleeves (2)
Using 3½-mm needles cast on 39 sts and work in single rib for 9 cm (3½ in) increasing in *every* st on last row (78 sts). Change to 4½-mm needles and work in diamond st as on back, increasing 1 st at each end of 9th and every following 8th row until there are 96 sts on needle. Then continue straight until sleeve is 48 cm (19 in) from beg. **Cast off** loosely.

Front band
Using 3½-mm needles cast on 9 sts and work in single rib. **1st row**: (*right side facing*) sl1, k1, *p1, k1, rep. from * to last st, k1 tbl. **2nd row**: sl1, *p1, k1, rep. from * to end. Repeat last 2 rows twice more. **Next 2 rows** (buttonhole rows): Rib 3, cast off 2 sts, rib to end. Rib to cast-off sts, cast on 2 sts, rib to end. Continue working in rib making further buttonholes at 8-cm (3-in) intervals till 6 in all have

been worked. Then carry on in rib until front band fits all round the front of the cardigan nicely – *very slightly stretched.* **Cast off** in rib.

Making up

Join shoulder seams. Set in sleeve by placing centre of sleeve top to shoulder seam – making sure that sleeve top lies nice and flat where joined to body. Join side and sleeve seams. Sew on front band, pinning centre of band to centre of back neck to ensure an even length of band up both sides of the cardigan. It is most important that the band should fit well as this makes the entire garment the right shape and gives it a good quality finish. Attach buttons to front band to correspond with buttonholes.

Double-knit classic cable sweater

Measurements Bust: 91 cm (36 in).
Length: 56 cm (22 in). Sleeve seam:
45 cm (17½ in)
Materials 15 × 25 gm balls of double-
knitting yarn and 2 small buttons for
shoulder opening
Needles A pair each of 3¼-mm (No. 10)
and 5-mm (No. 6)
Abbreviations See page 16
Tension 9 sts equal 5 cm (2 in) on 5-mm
needles

Front
With 3¼-mm needles cast on 62 sts and
work in single rib for 10 cm (4 in).
Change to 5-mm needles and work in
pattern. **1st row:** p1, *k8, p1, k1, p1, k1,
p1, rep. from * to last 9 sts, k8, p1. **2nd
row:** k1, * p8, k2, p1, k2, rep. from * to
last 9 sts, p8, k1. **3rd row:** p1, *k2, cable
4 thus; slip next 2 sts on cable needle and
leave at front of work, k2, then k2 from
cable needle, k2, p1, k1, p1, k1, p1. Rep.

from * to last 9 sts, k2, cable 4, k2, p1.
4th row: as 2nd. **5th row:** as 1st. **6th
row:** as 2nd. **7th row:** p1, *cable 4 twice,
p1, k1, p1, k1, p1, rep. from * to last 9
sts, cable 4 twice, p1. **8th row:** as 2nd.
Continue in pattern inc. 1 st at both ends
of next and every following 6th row till
there are 76 sts on needle, working extra
sts in moss st. Continue straight until
the work measures 37 cm (14½ in) ending
with right side facing. **Shape armholes:**
by casting off 4 sts at beg. of next 2 rows,
then dec. 1 st at both ends of every row
until 62 sts remain. Continue straight till
work measures 48 cm (19 in) ending with
right side facing. **Shape neck:** pattern
across 26 sts, cast off 10 sts, pattern to
end. Work on 2nd set of 26 sts for one
side of neck, dec. 1 st at neck edge on
every row till 18 sts remain. Continue
straight until work measures 56 cm (22 in)
ending at armhole edge. **Shape
shoulders:** cast off 6 sts at beginning of

next and following 2 alt. rows.
Rejoin yarn to remaining 26 sts and work to match.

Back
Work as for front until armhole shapings are completed and 62 sts remain. Continue straight until work measures 56 cm (22 in) ending with right side facing. **Shape shoulder and neck**: pattern 22 sts, cast off 18 sts, pattern to end. Work on last 22 sts. **Next row**: cast off 6 sts, pattern to last 2 sts, k2 tog. **Next row**: k2 tog. pattern to end. Repeat last 2 rows once more. **Cast off.** Rejoin yarn to remaining 22 sts, work to end then complete to match 1st side.

Sleeves (2)
With 3¼-mm needles cast on 39 sts and work in single rib for 6 cm (2½ in). On last row rib 15 sts, inc. in each of next 10 sts, rib 14 sts (49 sts). Change to 5-mm needles and work in pattern as for front inc. 1 st at each end of the 9th and every following 12th row until there are 59 sts on needle. Continue straight till sleeve measures 45 cm (17½ in). **Shape top**: dec. 1 st at both ends of next and every alt. row until 43 sts remain. Then dec. at both ends of every row until 21 sts remain. Cast off 2 sts at beg. of next 6 rows. **Cast off.**

Neckband
Join right shoulder seam. Using 3¼-mm needles and with right side of work facing, starting at left shoulder seam, pick up and knit 18 sts down front neck, 10 sts across centre front, 18 sts up other side of front neck, 6 sts down back neck, 18 sts across centre back, and 6 sts up other side of back neck (76 sts). Work in single rib for 6 cm (2½ in). **Cast off** loosely in rib.

Making up
Press lightly on the wrong side if yarn used is appropriate (see page 16). Join all seams except the left shoulder seam, which should be left open to within 3 cm (1¼ in) of armhole end. Sew in sleeves. Neatly

double crochet or blanket st opening in left shoulder, inserting 2 buttonholes and attaching buttons to correspond.

Note
Even the 1930s sporty look still hugged the figure. This sweater suits clear or even rich colours, i.e. rich denim blue, rust, gold, moss green – through to royal, red, burgundy, emerald, cerise, yellow, baltique (deep turquoise). To ring the changes with this sweater use yarn double – in which case increase size of needles to 4-mm and 6-mm, make underarm length 45 cm (17½ in) and overall length 66 cm (26 in) and you will have the modern, loose, long, crotch-length sweater to go with trousers. Remember that you will then need twice the amount of yarn.

KNITTING

Lace stitch and rib sweater

Measurements Bust: 84 cm (33 in)
Length – shoulder to lower edge: 52 cm
(20½ in). Sleeve seam: 45 cm (17½ in)
Materials 10 × 25 gm balls of 4-ply
yarn
Needles 1 pair each of 3¼-mm (No. 10)
and 4½-mm (No. 7) and a medium-size
crochet hook
Abbreviations See page 16
Tension 1 of the lace patterns equals
7 cm (2¾ in) across on 4½-mm needles

Back

With 3¼-mm needles cast on 96 sts and
work in single rib for 10 cm (4 in), knitting
twice into last st on last row (97 sts).
Change to 4½-mm needles and pattern
as follows: **1st row:** (right side of work)
sl1, p4, *k3, p4, p2 tog., m1, p5, rep. from
* to last 8 sts, k3, p4, k1 tbl. **2nd row:**
sl1, k4, *p3, k5, p1, k5, rep. from * to last
8 sts, p3, k4, k1 tbl. **3rd row:** sl1, p4, *k3,
p3, p2 tog., m1, k1, m1, p2 tog., p3, rep.
from * to last 8 sts, k3, p4, k1 tbl. **4th row:**
sl1, k4, *p3, k4, p3, k4, rep. from
* to last 8 sts, p3, k4, k1 tbl. **5th row:**
k1 *m1, p2 tog., p2, k3, p2 tog., m1,
k3, rep. from * finishing last rep. with k1
tbl instead of k3. **6th row:** sl1, p1, *k3,
p3, k3, p5, rep. from * finishing last rep.
with p1, k1 tbl instead of p5. **7th row:** sl1,
k1, *m1, p2 tog., p1, k3, p1, p2 tog., m1,
k5, rep. from * finishing last rep. with k1,
k1 tbl instead of k5. **8th row:** sl1, p2,
*k2, p3, k2, p7, rep. from * finishing last
rep. with p2, k1 tbl instead of p7. **9th
row:** sl1, k2, *m1, p2 tog., k3, p2 tog., m1,
k7, rep. from * finishing last rep. with k2,

k1 tbl instead of k7. **10th row:** sl1, k3,
*k1, p3, k1, p9, rep. from * finishing last
rep. with p3, k1 tbl instead of p9. **11th
row:** as 7th. **12th row:** as 8th. **13th row:**
as 5th. **14th row:** as 6th. **15th row:** as 3rd.
16th row: as 4th. These 16 rows form 1
complete pattern. Continue in pattern till
work measures 34 cm (13½ in). **Shape
armholes:** (taking care to keep continuity
of the pattern correct) by casting off 6sts
at beg. of next 2 rows, then dec. 1 st at
beg. of next 8 rows (77 sts). Continue in
pattern without further shaping until work
is 49 cm (19¼ in) from start. **Shape neck:**
pattern across 30 sts, cast off 17 sts,
pattern to end. Now continue to work on
last 30 sts. ****Next row:** pattern to last 2
sts, k2 tog. **Next row:** cast off 3 sts,
pattern to end. Rep. last 2 rows twice (18
sts). **Shape shoulder: ***1st and 3rd
rows:** cast off 5 sts, pattern to last 2 sts,
k2 tog. **2nd row:** k2 tog., pattern to end.
4th row: work pattern. **Cast off
remaining 5 sts.**** Join yarn to neck edge
of remaining sts, pattern 1 row, then work
this side to match 1st side from ** to **.

Front

Work as for back until armhole shapings
are completed. **Divide for front
opening:** pattern 26 sts, cast off 25 sts,
pattern to end. Working over last set of
26 sts continue in pattern until work
measures 49 cm (19¼ in) from start, then
dec. at neck edge on every row until 17 sts
remain. **Shape shoulder:** as given for
back from *** to **. Join yarn to neck

edge of remaining 26 sts and work this
side to match 1st side, but start neck
shaping 1 row sooner.

Sleeves (2)

With 3¼-mm needles cast on 41 sts and
work in single rib for 9 cm (3½ in). **Next
row**: k twice into first st, k1, *k twice
into next st, k2, rep. from * to end
(55 sts). Change to 4½-mm needles, work
in pattern as for back inc. 1 st at each end
of 17th row and then every 6th row until
there are 89 sts on needle. Continue until
sleeve measures 45 cm (17½ in) from beg.
Shape top: by casting off 2 sts at beg. of
next 2 rows. Then dec. 1 st at each end of
every row until 45 sts remain. Continue
without further shaping for 18 rows then
dec. 1 st at both ends of every row till
17 sts remain. **Cast off.**

Neckband

With 3¼-mm needles cast on 13 sts and
work in moss st. **Every row**: k1, * p1, k1,
rep. from * to end. Work for 43 cm
(17 in). **Cast off.**

Making up

Join all seams carefully. Sew moss st band
to neck, stitching the cast-on and cast-off
edges of band to straight edge of front
neck. Set sleeves into armholes, gathering
extra fullness at top of sleeve. Make a
crochet chain 51 cm (20 in) long and
thread through moss st band at front neck
for a tie. Press using appropriate method
(see page 16).

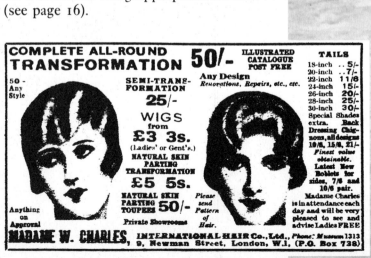

KNITTING

Sleeveless Jacquard cardigan

Measurements Bust: 86 [91, 97, 102] cm
(34 [36, 38, 40] in) Length: 66 [66, 70, 70]
cm (26 [26, 27½, 27½] in)

Materials Of 25 gm balls of double-
knitting yarn 7 balls in 0 (main colour),
3 balls each of colours 1, 2, 3 and 5,
2 balls of colour 4, plus 6 buttons to
match

Needles A pair each of 3½-mm (No. 9)
and 5-mm (No. 6)

Abbreviations See page 16

Tension 17 sts equal 8 cm (3 in) over
Jacquard pattern on 5-mm needles.

Back

With 3½-mm needles and double-knitting
yarn cast on 96 [104, 108, 112] sts and
work in single rib for 8 cm (3 in). Change
to 5-mm needles and work from 1st row
of Fair Isle chart till work measures
41 [41, 43, 43] cm (16 [16, 17, 17] in)
from beg. **Shape armhole:** by casting off
8 sts at beg. of next 2 rows still continuing
in Fair Isle (start from row 1 again when
you reach the end of the pattern). Then
continue straight until work measures
66 [66, 69, 70] cm (26 [26, 27, 27½] in).
Drop any other colours you are using at
this point and with main colour only cast
off 11 [12, 12, 13] sts at the beg. of
the next 6 rows. **Cast off** remaining sts.

Fronts (2)

First front: with 3½-mm needles cast on
44 [48, 48, 52] sts and work in single rib
for 8 cm (3 in). Change to 5-mm needles
and work from chart as for back until
work measures 41 [41, 43, 43] cm (16 [16,
17, 17] in) ending at armhole edge.

Shape armhole: cast off 8 sts, knit Fair
Isle to end. Continue straight for 2½ cm
(1 in) till work measures 43 [43, 46, 46] cm
(17 [17, 18, 18] in) from beg., finishing
at front edge.

Now start shaping front slope: k2 tog,
work to end. Work 3 rows straight. Repeat
these last 4 rows until 33 [36, 36, 39] sts
remain. Then continue straight until work
measures 66 [66, 69, 70] cm (26 [26, 27,
27½] in) ending at the armhole edge.

Shape shoulder: by dropping any other
colour so far used and working in main
colour only cast off 11 [12, 12, 13] sts at
the beg. of the next and following 2 alt.
rows. *Work other front reversing all
shapings.*

Front band

Using main colour and 3½-mm needles
cast on 13 sts. **1st row:** (right side facing)
sl1, k1 *p1, k1, rep. from * to last st, knit
into back of last st. **2nd row:** sl1, *p1, k1,
rep. from * to end. Rep. last 2 rows twice
more. **Next 2 rows:** (buttonhole rows)
Rib 5, cast off 2 sts, rib to end. Rib 5, cast
on 2 sts, rib to end. Continue working in
rib, making a further 5 buttonholes at
7 [7, 8, 8] cm (2½ [2½, 3, 3] in) intervals,
then repeat 1st and 2nd rows until band
fits – very slightly stretched – up left
front, across back neck and down right
side of garment. **Cast off.**

Making up

Sew up neatly, sewing in all ends and
using flatstitch or small oversewing. When
stitching on the front band, pin centre of

band to centre of back neck so that there is an even length of band up both sides of the cardigan. It is most important that the band should fit well – it makes the entire garment look much better and gives a quality finish.

Jacquard Fair Isle charts

row					row
70	0	0	0	0	
	0	0	0	0	69
68	0	0	0	0	
	0	0	0	3	67
66	3	0	3	3	
	3	3	3	4	65
64	4	3	4	4	
	3	3	3	4	63
62	3	3	3	4	
	3	5	3	3	61
60	5	5	5	3	
	3	5	3	3	59
58	3	5	3	3	
	3	3	3	4	57
56	4	3	4	4	
	3	3	3	4	55
54	0	0	0	3	
	0	0	0	3	53
52	0	0	0	0	
	0	0	0	0	51
50	2	1	1	2	
	2	2	1	1	49
48	1	2	2	1	
	1	1	2	2	47
46	2	1	1	2	
	2	2	1	1	45
44	3	3	3	3	
	3	3	3	3	43
42	4	4	4	4	
	4	4	4	4	41
40	0	0	0	0	
	0	0	0	5	39
38	5	0	5	0	
	2	5	2	2	37

row					row
36	2	2	2	0	
	0	2	0	0	35
34	2	2	2	0	
	2	5	2	2	33
32	5	0	5	0	
	0	0	0	5	31
30	0	0	0	0	
	3	4	3	3	29
28	4	4	4	3	
	3	4	3	3	27
26	4	4	4	3	
	3	4	3	4	25
24	0	0	0	0	
	0	0	0	0	23
22	2	2	2	2	
	2	2	2	2	21
20	1	1	1	1	
	1	1	1	2	19
18	2	1	2	1	
	1	2	1	2	17
16	2	2	2	1	
	2	2	2	2	15
14	2	2	2	0	
	0	2	0	2	13
12	2	0	2	0	
	0	0	0	2	11
10	0	0	0	0	
	0	0	0	1	9
8	1	0	1	0	
	0	1	0	1	7
6	1	1	1	0	
	1	1	1	1	5
4	2	2	2	2	
	2	2	2	2	3
2	1	1	1	1	
	1	1	1	1	1

Some suggested colour combinations

0: raspberry
1: navy
2: pink
3: beige
4: airforce blue (greyish blue)
5: navy

0: camel
1: black
2: cream
3: grey
4: gold
5: black

0: natural
1: grey
2: gold
3: chocolate
4: rust
5: grey

0: grey
1: burgundy
2: natural
3: black
4: airforce blue (greyish blue)
5: burgundy

0: navy
1: rust
2: cream
3: rich brown
4: grey
5: rust

0: red
1: navy
2: cream
3: grey
4: teal blue (deep aqua)
5: yellow

Here's CHIC and GOOD TASTE

MATERIALS

Sirdar Super Shetland Wool, 3-ply, 4 oz. light; 1 oz. dark (for the long sleeves an extra 2 oz. of light wool will be required).
2 Abel Morrall's Aero knitting pins, No. 8.
3 patent fasteners.   3 buttons.   A buckle.

To obtain the best results it is essential that you use the materials exactly as mentioned above.

MEASUREMENTS

Shoulder to lower edge, 18½ inches; short sleeve seam, 4½ inches; long sleeve seam, 18 inches. To fit a 33-34 inch bust.

Abbreviations.—K., knit; p., purl; tog., together; st., stitch; m.s., moss-stitch—knit 1, purl 1, to end of row, always commencing next row with same kind of stitch as last row finished with; knit 2 into next—by knitting into back as well as front of stitch before slipping it off needle.

Always knit into back of each cast-on stitch.

Tension of moss-stitch about 7 stitches and 9½ rows to one inch.

THE LOWER BACK and FRONT ALIKE

Using light wool, commence at lower edge, casting on 100 stitches. Knit in ribbing of k. 1, p. 1, for 11½ inches. Cast off.

THE BACK YOKE

USING light wool, commence at lower edge, casting on 100 stitches. **1st row**—K. 1, p. 1, alt. to end. **2nd row**—P. 1, k. 1, alt. to end. Now shape armholes. **Next 8 rows**—K. 2 tog., knit in m.s. until 2 remain, k. 2 tog. (84 stitches). Knit in m.s. until back measures 6¼ inches. Now shape shoulders. **Next 6 rows**—Cast off 8, knit in m.s. to end (36 stitches). Cast off.

THE FRONT YOKE (both sides alike)

Using light wool, commence at lower edge, casting on 54 stitches. Knit 2 rows m.s. Now shape armholes. **Next row**—K. 2 tog., knit in m.s. to end. **Next row**—Knit in m.s. until 2 remain, k. 2 tog. Repeat last 2 rows 3 times (46 stitches). Knit in m.s. until front measures 5½ inches finishing last row at opposite edge from armhole shaping. Now shape for neck. **Next row**—Cast off 16, knit in m.s. to end. **Next row**—Knit in m.s. until 2 remain, k. 2 tog. **Next row**—K. 2

Here you see the exact size of the moss-stitch which is used for the back and front of the yoke.

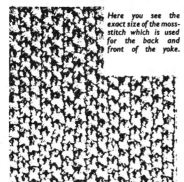

tog., knit in m.s. to end. Repeat last 2 rows twice (24 stitches). Knit in m.s. until front measures 6½ inches, finishing last row at opposite edge of neck shaping. **Next row**—Cast off 6, knit in m.s. to end. **Next row**—Knit in m.s. Repeat last 2 rows twice (6 stitches). Cast off.

THE SHORT SLEEVES (both alike)

Using light wool, commence at lower edge, casting on 72 stitches. Knit in m.s. for **4 rows. Next row**—K. 2 into next st., knit in m.s. until 1 remains, k. 2 into last st. Repeat these 5 rows 5 times (84 stitches). **Next 2 rows**—Knit in m.s. Now shape top. **Next 36 rows**—K. 2 tog., knit in m.s. until 2 remain, k. 2 tog. (12 stitches). Cast off.

THE LONG SLEEVES (both alike)

Using light wool, commence at lower edge, casting on 56 stitches. Knit in m.s. for 9 rows. **10th row**—K. 2 into first st., knit in m.s. until 1 remains, k. 2 into last st. Repeat these 10 rows 13 times (84 stitches). Knit in m.s. until sleeve measures 17 inches. Now shape top. **Next 36 rows**—K. 2 tog., knit in m.s. until 2 remain, k. 2 tog. (12 stitches). Cast off.

THE FRONT TAB

Using light wool, cast on 14 stitches. Knit in m.s. for 4½ inches. **Next row**—K. 2 tog., knit in m.s. until 2 remain, k. 2 tog. Repeat last row until all stitches are worked off.

THE COLLAR (both sides alike)

. Using dark wool, cast on 30 stitches. Knit in m.s. for 7 inches. Cast off.

THE SLEEVES BANDS (both alike)

Using dark wool, cast on 7 stitches. Knit in m.s. for 16 inches. Cast off.

Isn't this a lovely little Jumper? It is very easy to knit and so charming in primrose and brown; Margaret Rose and brown; navy and white, or scarlet and white.

Directions are given for both long and short sleeves—the long ones can easily be added to your jumper when the cooler autumn days come.

THE BELT

Using dark wool, cast on 18 stitches. Knit in ribbing of k. 1, p. 1, for 28 inches. **Next row**—K. 2 tog., knit in rib until 2 remain, k. 2 tog. Repeat last row until all stitches are worked off.

TO MAKE UP

Pin out each piece and press on wrong side under a damp cloth with a hot iron. Sew back yoke to lower part of jumper, then sew front yokes to lower part, allowing the right side to overlap the left side at centre front for about ½ an inch. Sew up underarm, shoulder and sleeve seams. Sew in sleeves, placing seam level with underarm. Sew bands to lower edge of sleeves, tying ends as seen in illustration. Sew front tab to right side of front opening. Sew on buttons and fasteners. Sew on both pieces of collar making the ends come to centre back and front. Sew buckle to straight end of belt. Press all seams.

PLEASE NOTE

It is always advisable to read through the instructions several times before commencing the garment, to get a general idea of its structure.

Throughout these knitting instructions when decreasings are made by casting off, the stitch remaining on the right-hand needle after casting off is included in the number of stitches quoted immediately after.

The asterisks (or stars) in the instructions denote the points from which the directions are repeated.

It is important to knit at the correct tension. Knit up a small square and test. If tension is too loose, use smaller needles or the garment will not be the size specified.

KNITTING

4-ply lumber jacket

Measurements (*after pressing*) Bust:
94 cm (37 in). Length from lower edge to
shoulder: 51 cm (20 in). Sleeve seam:
45 cm (17½ in)
Materials 14 × 25 gm balls of 4-ply
yarn in main colour, 1 ball in first contrast
and 1 ball in second contrast, 12 small
buttons and a snap-fastener
Needles A pair each of 2½-mm (No. 12)
and 3¼-mm (No. 10)
Abbreviations See page 16
Tension 7 sts and 10 rows make a square
of 2½ cm (1 in) using 3¼-mm needles

Back
With 2½-mm needles cast on 124 sts in
main colour and work in single rib for 36
rows. Change to 3¼-mm needles and work
in stocking st for 90 rows. **Shape
armholes:** cast off 3 sts at beg. of next 6
rows and then k2 tog. at beg. of each of
the following 20 rows (86 sts). Work 40
rows straight. **Cast off** loosely.

Left front
Pocket lining: with 3¼-mm needles cast
on 24 sts in main colour and work 45 rows
in stocking st leaving this work on a spare
needle for the time being. Now commence
front by casting on 72 sts with 2½-mm
needles in main colour. **1st row:** *k1, p1,
rep. from * until 10 sts remain, p7, k3.
2nd row: k10, k1, p1, rib to end. Repeat
last 2 rows until 36 rows have been
worked and then change to 3¼-mm needles
and proceed as follows: **37th row:** all purl
until 3 sts remain, k3. **38th row:** knit.
Repeat the last 2 rows until 122 rows have

been worked from edge. ****123rd row:**
p19, transfer the next 24 sts to a large
safety-pin or stitch-holder and, with
pocket lining wrong side facing, purl the
24 sts from spare needle, p26, k3. **124th
row:** knit. **125th row:** purl to last 3 sts,
k3. **126th row:** knit. **Shape armhole:**
cast off 3 sts, purl to last 3 sts, k3. **Next
row:** knit. Repeat last 2 rows twice more.
Next row: k2 tog., purl to last 3 sts, k3.
Next row: knit. Repeat last 2 rows 9
times more (54 sts). Repeat 37th and 38th
rows 6 times more. **Next row:** purl to last
3 sts, k3. **To shape neck:** cast off 10 sts,
knit to end. Continue in stocking st and
k2 tog. at the neck edge on *every* row until
24 sts remain. Work for a further 18
rows on these sts. **Cast off** *loosely*.
Now pick up 24 sts from stitch-holder and
with 2½-mm needles and wrong side facing,
in main colour continue on the 24 sts as
follows: **1st row:** *k2, inc. in next st, rep.
from * to end (32 sts). **2nd row:** k1, p1,
rib to end. **3rd row:** knit (with 1st
contrast) **4th row:** k1, p1, rib to end (with
1st contrast). Rep. 3rd and 4th rows until
a further 7 stripes have been worked,
commencing with 2 rows in main colour
followed by 2 rows in 2nd contrast, 2 rows
in main colour, 2 rows in 1st contrast and
so on. **Cast off** *ribwise* with colour used
for last stripe.

Right front
Pocket lining: work as for left front, but
working for 44 rows only. Then with
2½-mm needles commence right front by
casting on 72 sts in main colour. **1st row:**

k3, p7 *k1, p1 rep. from * to end. **2nd row**: *k1, p1 rep. from * to end. Rep. last 2 rows once more. **5th row**: k3, p2, cast off 3 sts (1 st now on needle) p1 then k1, p1, rib to end. **6th row**: *k1, p1, rep from * until 7 sts remain k2, cast on 3 sts, k5. Rep. rows 1 and 2 until 36 rows in all have been worked from beg. inserting buttonhole rows 5 and 6 every 13th and 14th row from last buttonhole. Change to 3¼-mm needles and work as follows (remember to insert buttonhole as before until 12 in all have been completed – at this stage you will be within 9 rows of neck shaping): **1st row**: k3, purl to end. **2nd row**: all knit. Rep. last 2 rows until 123 rows in all have been worked from lower edge. Now repeat from ** on left front, except that a purl row becomes a knit row and vice versa. When 54 sts remain on needle repeat 1st and 2nd rows 14 more times and then continue to match other front.

Sleeves (2)

With 2½-mm needles cast on 50 sts in second contrast and work in single rib for 2 rows. ***Join in main colour. **3rd row**: knit. **4th row**: rib. Work 11 stripes in all, following method and colour sequence used on pocket tops. Then continue in main colour only: *k1, inc. in next st, rep from * to end (75 sts). Change to 3¼-mm needles and proceed as follows: **1st row**: knit. **2nd row**: purl. Continue in stocking st, inc. 1 st at both ends of every 10th row till there are 100 sts on needle. Work straight until work measures 45 cm (17½ in). **Shape top**: k2 tog. at both ends of every row until 16 sts remain. **Cast off** working 2 sts tog. all along the row.

Neckband

With 2½-mm needles cast on 130 sts in 2nd contrast and work exactly as for cuff (18 rows in all). **Cast off** loosely.

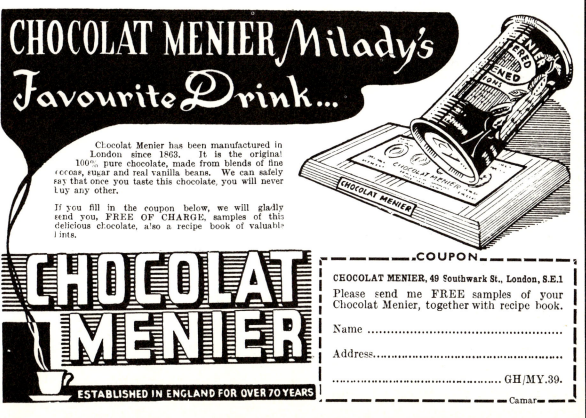

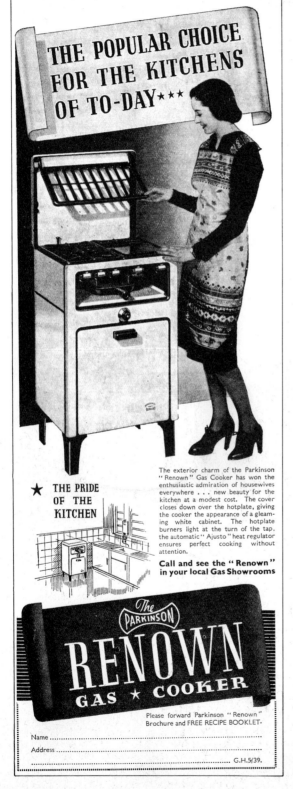
Making up

Seam up shoulders and sew tops of sleeves into armholes. Neatly hem in the border of 3 garter sts along fronts. While still open carefully press (refer to page 16 for method) over the knit side of the work. Sew up sleeve and side seams in one operation and sew cast-off edge of neckband to neck opening. Sew pocket edgings in place and press all seams (if yarn used is suitable).

Now, on both fronts, beginning immediately above the ribbing and in line with centre of pocket edging, pick up yarn through every 3rd st with 1st contrast, up to pocket edging. On each side of 1st contrast line work a 2nd contrast line using the same method but substituting 2 sts instead of 3 sts. Sew on buttons to correspond with buttonholes and fasten neck with a snap-fastener.

Suggested colour combinations

main colour: grey
1st contrast: rust
2nd contrast: yellow

main colour: burgundy
1st contrast: light beige
2nd contrast: red

main colour: chocolate brown
1st contrast: airforce blue (greyish blue)
2nd contrast: cream

main colour: cream
1st contrast: grey
2nd contrast: gold

main colour: camel
1st contrast: black
2nd contrast: cream

main colour: navy
1st contrast: cream
2nd contrast: rust

main colour: natural
1st contrast: camel
2nd contrast: black

IN THESE DAYS OF STRICT ECONOMY

it is wise to use Femina Wools. Women are fortunate to have at their disposal a range of knitting wools which combine the latest trends of fashion with excellent wearing qualities, and at a very reasonable price. The varied and wide choice of smart colours is, of course, supported by Khaki, Navy, and Air Force Blue.

Femina
KNITTING WOOLS

IN CASE OF DIFFICULTY WRITE TO BAIRNS-WEAR LIMITED, DEPT. C.117, HUCKNALL ROAD, NOTTINGHAM.

KNITTING

Knot stitch sweater with round yoke

Measurements Bust: 86 [91] cm
(34 [36] in). Length: 37 cm (14½ in).
Sleeve seam: 45 cm (17½ in)
Materials 11 [12] × 25 gm balls of 4-ply
yarn and 4 small buttons to match
Needles A pair each of 2½-mm (No. 12),
3½- [4-] mm (No. 9 [No. 8]) plus a
medium-size crochet hook
Abbreviations See page 16
Tension 13 sts equal 5 cm (2 in) on
3½-mm needles

Note
To make knot (mk), p3 tog., leave sts on
left-hand needle, wrn, p into same 3 sts.

Back
Using 2½-mm needles cast on 111 sts and
work in single rib for 9 cm (3½ in).
Change to 3½- [4-] mm needles and pattern
as follows: work in stocking st for 8 rows.
9th row: sl1, *k11, mk, rep. from * to last
12 sts, k11, k1 tbl. Work 9 rows in
stocking st. **19th row:** sl1, p1, k4, * mk,
k11, rep. from * to last 7 sts, mk, k4, k1
tbl. Work 9 rows in stocking st. These last
20 rows from row 9 to 28 inclusive form
the basic pattern which repeats
throughout. Work straight until work
measures 36 cm (14 in). **Shape
shoulders:** by casting off 3 sts at the beg.
of the next 8 rows, then 2 sts at beg. of
the next 2 rows (83 sts). Work 14 rows
without shaping, *all the time keeping
pattern correct.* **Divide for yoke:** by
working across 41 sts, turn, leaving
the remaining sts for 2nd half. **2nd row:**
cast off 3 sts, pattern to end. **3rd row:**

work in pattern. Rep. last 2 rows until 2
sts remain. Work these 2 sts tog. on last
row and draw yarn through remaining st
and fasten off. Rejoin yarn to remaining
42 sts and work to match 1st side of yoke,
reversing shapings.

Front
Work same as back but knit only 4 rows
of those 14 rows worked straight
immediately after armhole shaping, so
yoke shaping starts 4 rows after last
armhole shaping row.

Sleeves (2)
Using 2½-mm needles cast on 50 sts and
work in single rib for 35 rows. **36th row:**
rib 15, inc. in each of the next 19 sts, rib
16 (69 sts). Change to 3½- [4-] mm needles
and work in pattern for 2 complete
patterns. Then inc. at each end of the
next and every following 8th row 5 times
(79 sts), working inc. sts in plain stocking
st. Continue straight until work measures
45 cm (17½ in) inc. in last st of last row
(80) sts. **Shape top of sleeve:** cast off 3
sts at beg. of next 4 rows, then dec. 1 st at
each end of every other row until 32 sts
remain. Work 15 rows straight. **Next row:**
p2 tog. all along row (16) sts – leave these
on a safety-pin to pick up for yoke. **Yoke:**
using 3½- [4-] mm needles with right side
facing and starting at centre back, pick up
43 sts on left side of back, 16 sts from
sleeve, 86 sts evenly round front (43 from
each side of front), 16 sts from next sleeve
and 43 sts from right side of back (204 sts).
2nd row: (*wrong side*) sl1, *p4, k2,

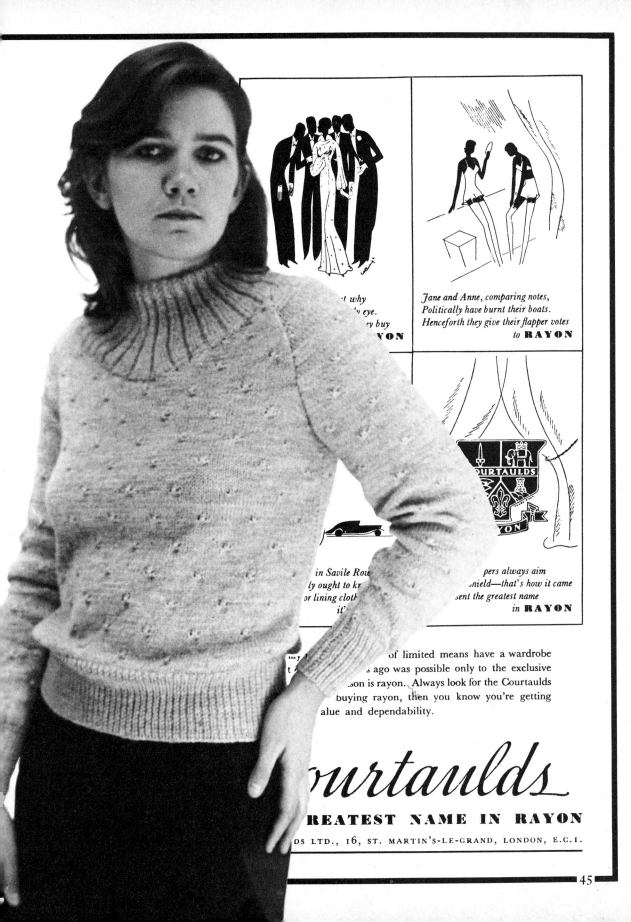

rep. from * ending with a k1 tbl instead of k2. **3rd row**: sl 1, *k4, p2, rep. from * ending k4, k1 tbl. Work 9 more rows in rib as set. **Next row**: sl1, *sl1, k1, psso, k2, p2, rep. from * ending last rep. with k1 tbl (instead of p2). **Next row**: sl1, *p3, k2, rep. from * to end, ending last rep. with k1 tbl (instead of k2). Work 10 more rows in rib as set (k3, p2 on right side). **Next row**: sl1, *k1, k2 tog., p2, rep from * ending last rep. with k1 tbl (instead of p2). **Next row**: sl1, *p2, k2, rep. from * ending k1 tbl. Work 10 more rows in rib as set (k2, p2 on right side). **Next row**: sl1, k2, *p2 tog., k2, rep. from * to last st, k1 tbl. **Next row**: sl1, *p2, k1, rep. from * to end. Work 7 more rows in same rib. **Cast off**: work tog. every 2nd and 3rd st.

Shoulder pads (2) (optional)
With 3½-mm needles cast on 14 sts and work in single rib for 10 cm (4 in). **Cast off**. Roll pad pieces widthwise forming rolls 2½ cm (1 in) wide. Stitch these under sleeve top at the centre, passing the sts up and down through one long end of the pad and through top sleeve seam.

Making up
Sew sleeves into armholes putting any extra fullness at top. Join side and sleeve seams in one line. Work row of double crochet or blanket st around back yoke opening making 3 loop buttonholes, and then attach buttons to correspond with buttonholes.

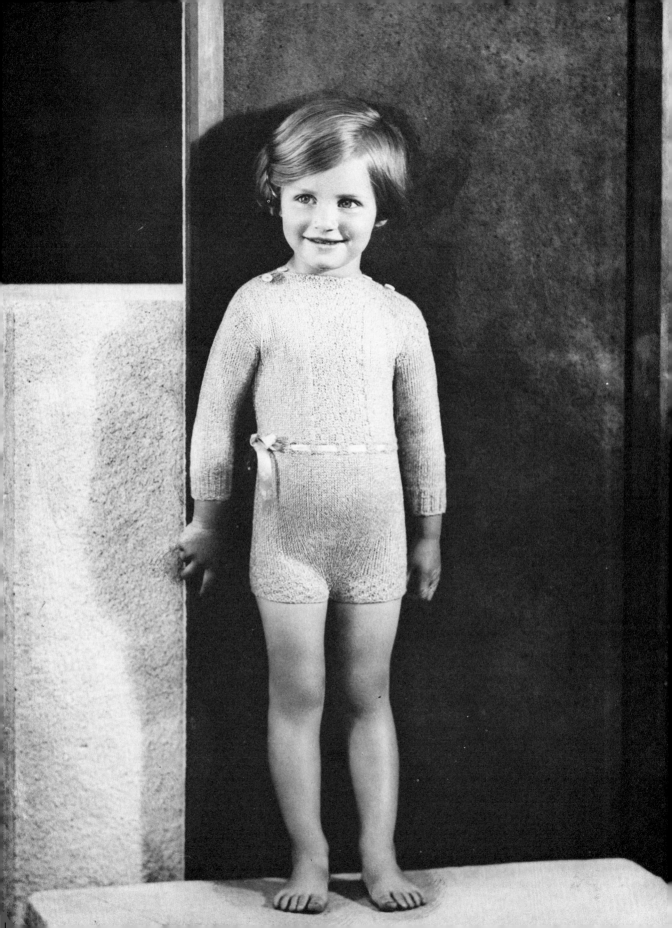

Lacy 'V' neck sweater

Measurements (To fit loosely) Bust:
86 [91, 97] cm (34 [36, 38] in). Length:
67 [69, 69] cm (26½ [27, 27]) Sleeve seam:
46 [48, 51] cm (18 [19, 20] in)
Materials 24 × 25 gm balls of double-
knitting yarn
Needles A pair each of 3¼-mm (No. 10),
4-mm (No. 8) and 5-mm (No. 6)
Abbreviations See page 16
Tension 11 sts of pattern equal 5 cm (2
in) using 5-mm needles

Back

Using 3¼-mm needles cast on 88 [96, 104]
sts and work in single rib for 9 cm (3½ in)
increasing 1 st at each end of last row of
rib 90 [98, 106] sts. Change to 5-mm
needles and work lace st as follows: sl1, k1
[ko, ko],*k1, wl.fwd, k2 tog., rep. from * to
last st, k1 tbl (on largest size repeat from
* to end). This one row is the pattern.
Just repeat throughout being very
careful to keep the pattern correct
when you come to shaped parts (raglan
and 'V' neck) and make sure that the
lines of the pattern are not broken
– the ridge must be straight. Continue
working straight until work measures
43 [45, 45] cm (17[17½,17½]in) from start
finishing with right side facing. **Shape
raglan:** cast off 4 [4, 5] sts at beg. of the
next 2 rows. **3rd row:** sl1, k2 tog., pattern
to last 3 sts, k2 tog., k1 tbl. **4th row:** sl1
k2 tog., pattern to last 3 sts, k2 tog., k1
tbl. For the larger size rep. last 2 rows twice
more. *All sizes:* **Next row:** sl1, k2 tog.,
pattern to last 3 sts, k2 tog., k1 tbl. **Next
row:** sl1, pattern to last st, k1 tbl. **Rep.**

last 2 rows until 26 [26, 28] sts remain.
Leave these sts on a spare needle to pick
up for the neckband.

Fronts (2)

Work as for back to beg. of raglan shaping.
Raglan and 'V' neck shaping: cast
off 4 [4, 5] sts, pattern until 41 [45, 48] sts
are on the needle, *turn* and pattern
back. **3rd row:** sl1, k2 tog., pattern to last
st, k1 tbl. **4th row:** sl1, k2 tog., pattern to
last 3 sts, k2 tog., k1 tbl. For the larger
size work the raglan shaping on *every* row
for the next 4 rows, and then continue the
raglan shaping on every *alt.* row as on
back. For the 2 smaller sizes go straight
into shaping raglan on every *alt.* row and
on *all sizes* dec. 1st, as on 4th row, on
every 4th row 10 more times (11 decreases
in all on the neck side). Then stop
shaping the neck side and just carry on
shaping the raglan until 2 sts remain.
Fasten off. Work second half to match
first half of front, *reversing shapings.*

Sleeves (2)

Using 3¼-mm needles cast on 39 [39, 41]
sts and work in single rib for 9 cm (3½ in)
increasing in *every* st on the last row of
welt 78 [78, 82] sts. Change to 5-mm
needles and pattern increasing at each end
of 9th and every following 8th row until
there are 90 [98, 106] sts on needle. Then
continue straight until work measures
46 [48, 51] cm (18 [19, 20] in) from start
finishing with right side facing. **Shape
raglan:** cast off 6 [6, 8] sts at beg. of the
next 2 rows. **3rd row:** sl1, k2 tog., pattern

to last 3 sts, k2 tog., k1 tbl. **4th row**: sl1, k2 tog., pattern to last 3 sts, k2 tog., k1 tbl. Rep. last 2 rows 7 times more and then continue to shape raglan on every *alt*. (right side) row as on back until there are 8 sts left. Leave these sts on spare needle to pick up for the neckband.

Making up and neckband
Carefully sew up side and sleeve seams. Leaving the left back raglan seam open, join up the 3 other raglan shapings using a flatseam and joining notches. Then with 4-mm needles and right side of work facing pick up 8 sts from top of left sleeve, 52 [52, 56] sts down left side of neck, 1st from centre 'V' – marking this st with a piece of coloured thread as you will be decreasing on either side of this st on every row – 52 [52, 56] sts up right side of front neck, 8 sts from top of right sleeve and 26 [26, 28] sts from back. Now work 7 rows of single rib decreasing 1 st at each side of centre front neck (marked with coloured thread) on *every* row. **Cast off** *loosely* in rib. Join remaining raglan sleeve and neckband. *Do not press* as it would spoil appearance of stitch.

KNITTING

Lacy hat and scarf

Measurements Scarf is approximately 18 cm (7 in) wide and 183 cm (72 in) long, plus fringe and hat is average size
Materials 10 × 25 gm balls of double-knitting yarn
Needles A pair of $4\frac{1}{2}$-mm (No. 7), $5\frac{1}{2}$-mm (No. 5) and 6-mm (No. 4)
Abbreviations See page 16
Tension Approximately 3 patterns and 14 rows equal a square of 5 cm (2 in) on 6-mm needles

Scarf (not shown)
Using 5-mm needles cast on 30 sts and work 6 rows in garter st. Change to pattern. **Pattern row:** k3, *k1, wl.fwd, k2 tog., rep. from * to last 3 sts, k3. Rep. this single pattern row until scarf measures 183 cm (72 in), then work 6 rows in garter st. **Cast off.**

Fringe
Cut yarn into lengths of 31 cm (12 in) and taking 6 strands together knot along each end of the scarf – making 10 fringes at each end. A lovely thick fringe makes all the difference to the appearance of the garment.

Hat
With $4\frac{1}{2}$-mm needles and using yarn *double* cast on 74 sts and work 4 rows in single rib. Change to 6-mm needles and work in pattern. **Pattern row:** k1, *k1, wl.fwd, k2 tog., rep. from * to last st, k1. Rep. this single pattern row until work measures 14 cm ($5\frac{1}{2}$ in) from beg. **Shape crown:**

as follows working in garter st **1st row:** k1, *k6, k2 tog., rep. from * to last st, k1. **2nd and alt. rows:** knit. **3rd row:** k1, *k5, k2 tog., rep. from * to last st, k1. **5th row:** k1, *k4, k2 tog., rep. from * to last st, k1. **7th row:** k1, *k3, k2 tog., rep. from * to last st, k1. **9th row:** k1, *k2, k2 tog., rep. from * to last st, k1. **11th row:** k1, *k1, k2 tog., rep. from * to last st, k1. **12th row:** k2 tog., all along the row, then draw yarn through remaining stitches. **Fasten off** and sew up the back seam taking care not to pull the seam tight. *Do not press* either hat or scarf as it would spoil appearance of stitch.

KNITTING

Woman's Tyrolean-style cardigan

Measurements Bust: 83 [88] cm
(32½ [34½] in). Length: 50 cm (19½ in).
Sleeve seam: 45 cm (17½ in)
Materials 16 × 25 gm balls of double-knitting wool and oddments if you wish to add the simple embroidery, plus 4 buttons to match
Needles A pair each of 3½-mm (No. 9) and 5-mm (No. 6)
Abbreviations See page 16
Tension 9 sts equal 5 cm (2 in) using 5-mm needles

Note
To make woolly ball or bobble (mb) p1, k1, p1, k1 into st, making 4 sts out of this st. Turn, k4, turn, p4, sl 2nd, 3rd, 4th sts over 1st st.

Right front
Using 3½-mm needles cast on 34 [38] sts and work in single rib for 9 cm (3½ in). Change to 5-mm needles and proceed in pattern as follows: **1st row:** k23 (p1, k3) 2 [3] times, p1, k2. **2nd and alternate rows:** (p3, k1) 3 [4] times, p22. **3rd row:** k2, mb, k18 (p1, k3) 3 [4] times, p1. **5th row:** k4, mb, k18 (p1, k3) 2 [3] times, p1, k2. **7th row:** k2, mb, k3, mb, k14 (p1, k1) 3 [4] times, p1. **9th row:** k8, mb, k14 (p1, k3) 2 [3] times, p1, k2. **11th row:** k2, mb, k7, mb, k10 (p1, k3) 3 [4] times, p1. **13th row:** k5, mb, k6, mb, k3, mb, k6 (p1, k3) 2 [3] times, p1, k2. **15th row:** as 11th. **17th row:** as 9th. **19th row:** as 7th. **21st row:** as 5th. **23rd row:** as 3rd. **24th row:** as 2nd. These 24 rows form the pattern. Repeat pattern once more, then work 1st

row of pattern again, keeping the pattern correct. **Shape armhole:** by casting off 6 sts at beg. of next row (row 2 of pattern) then decrease 1 st at armhole edge on every row until 24 [28] sts remain. Continue until armhole measures 19 cm (7½ in) finishing at armhole edge. **Shape shoulder:** by casting off 9 [11] sts at beg. of next row. Work 1 row. **Next row:** cast off 3 [5] sts then work 2 sts tog. as you cast off rest of row.

Left front
Work to match right front, reversing all shapings and noting pattern rows to be read from end to beginning, i.e. **1st row:** k2, p1 (k3, p1) 2 [3] times, k23. **2nd and alternate rows:** p22 (k1, p3) 3 [4] times. **3rd row:** p1 (k3, p1) 3 [4] times, k18, mb, k2 and so on.

Back
Using 3½-mm needles cast on 72 [80] sts and work in single rib for 9 cm (3½ in) inc. 1 st at the end of last row. Change to 5-mm needles and work pattern. **1st row:** *k3, p1 rep. from * to last st, k1. **2nd and 4th rows:** p2 *k1, p3 rep. from * to last 3 sts, k1, p2. **3rd row:** k1 *p1, k3 rep. from * to end. These 4 rows form the pattern. Continue in pattern till work measures same as fronts up to armhole shaping, keeping the pattern correct. **Shape armholes:** by casting off 4 sts at beg. of next 2 rows, then dec. 1 st at each end of every row till 59 [63] sts remain. Continue pattern till work measures same as fronts to shoulder. **Shape shoulders:**

THEY USE UP ENERGY *so quickly...*

Active youngsters expend energy so lavishly. Yet they've two important jobs to do: they must grow and they must put on strength at the same time. Delicious Kellogg's Corn Flakes can help them do both. Serve them for breakfast, lunch or supper with cold milk or cream or with fruit as an extra treat.

The natural food element in Kellogg's Corn Flakes nourishes and sustains. Everybody thrives on Kellogg's Corn Flakes — kept oven-fresh by the exclusive inside WAXTITE wrapper. Ten generous helpings in each packet — crammed with food value. Ready to serve at a moment's notice. Sold by all grocers.

NOW ONLY

6D PER PKT

(Not I.F.S.)

Kellogg's
CORN
FLAKES
OVEN-FRESH
FLAVOUR-PERFECT

Kellogg's CORN FLAKES

Made by KELLOGG *in* LONDON, CANADA

930

THE BIGGEST VALUE IN CEREALS

54

by casting off 9 [11] sts at beg. of next 4 rows. **Cast off remaining sts.**

Sleeves (2)

Using 3½-mm needles cast on 39 sts and work in single rib for 9 cm (3½ in) inc. 1 st at each end of last row (41 sts). Change to 5-mm needles and proceed in pattern as for back, inc. 1 st at both ends of 5th and every following 6th row until there are 67 sts on the needle. Continue straight until sleeve is 45 cm (17½ in) from start. **Shape top:** (keeping pattern correct) by casting off 3 sts at beg. of next 4 rows then dec. 1 st at both ends of every row till 45 sts remain, then at both ends of every alternate row until 35 sts remain and finally at both ends of every 3rd row until 23 sts remain. Cast off 4 sts at beg. of next 4 rows. **Cast off.**

Front band

Using 3½-mm needles cast on 9 sts. **1st row:** k2 (p1, k1) 3 times, k1. **2nd row:** (k1, p1) 4 times, k1. **3rd and 4th rows:** as 1st and 2nd. **5th row:** Rib 4, wl.fwd, k2 tog., rib 3. **6th row:** rib. Continue in rib making buttonhole 15th row from previous buttonhole until 4 buttonholes have been made. **Cast off** when band fits nicely up front of cardigan (very slightly stretched) across back of neck and down left side of cardigan.

Making up

Using overstitch or flatstitch join shoulder seams and then attach front band. To make sure both sides match in length pin centre of front band to centre of back (neck) before sewing band to garment. Join other seams and sew in sleeves. Attach buttons to correspond with buttonholes.

Note

The addition of some very simple embroidery, such as the white petals illustrated, adds to the charm of this delightfully attractive cardigan.

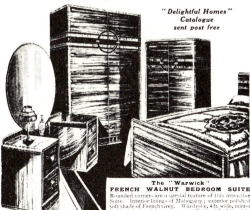

KNITTING

Tyrolean-style waistcoat

Measurements Bust: 83 [88] cm
(32½ [34½] in). Length: 50 cm (19½ in)
Materials 11 × 25 gm balls of double-knitting wool or similar weight yarn and oddments of wool for embroidery (optional), plus 4 buttons to match.
Needles A pair each of 3½-mm (No. 9) and 5-mm (No. 6)
Abbreviations See page 16
Tension 9 sts equals 5 cm (2 in) using 5-mm needles

Right front
Work as for right front of cardigan up to armhole shaping. **Work armhole band:** by working 7 sts in garter stitch at armhole end of every row, keeping this edge straight. Continue until armhole measures 19 cm (7½ in). **Shape shoulder:** by casting off 16 [18] sts at beg. of next row. Work 1 row. **Next row:** cast off 3 [5] sts. **Cast off,** working 2 sts tog. all along row.

Left front
Work to match right front, reversing all shapings and noting change in pattern rows (reading from end to beg.) as on cardigan.

Back
Work as for back of cardigan up to armhole shaping. Work in armhole bands by working 7 sts in garter st at each end of every row, keeping pattern correct, and working straight till work measures 19 cm (7½ in) from start of armbands. **Shape shoulders:** by casting off 16 [18] sts at

beg. of next 2 rows and 9 [11] sts at beg. of next 2 rows. **Cast off** remaining stitches.

Front band
Work as for cardigan.

Making up
Finish as for cardigan.

KNITTING

Man's 'V' neck cable sweater

Measurements Chest: 97 [102, 107] cm (38 [40,42] in). Length: 71 cm (28 in). Sleeve seam: (adjustable) 48 cm (19 in)
Materials 23 [24, 25] × 25 gm balls of double-knitting yarn
Needles A pair each of 2½-mm (No. 12), 3-mm (No. 11) and 4½-mm (No. 7)
Abbreviations See page 16
Tension 11 sts equal 5 cm (2 in) using 4½-mm needles

Note
To cable 4 sts (c4), sl 4 sts on to a cable needle, leave at front of work, k4, then k4 from cable needle.

Back
With 2½-mm needles cast on 110 [116, 122] sts and work in single rib for 9 cm (3½ in). **Next row:** rib 5 [8, 6] sts (inc. in next st, rib 10 [10, 11]) 9 times, inc. in next stitch, rib to end 120 [126, 132] sts. Change to 4½-mm needles and stocking st in cable pattern: **1st and 3rd rows:** (k10 [11, 12] p2, k8, p2), 5 times, k10 [11, 12]. **2nd and every alt. row:** (p10 [11, 12], k2, p8, k2) 5 times, p10 [11, 12]. **5th row:** (k10 [11, 12] p2, c4, p2) 5 times, k10 [11, 12]. **7th and 9th rows:** as 1st row. **10th row:** as 2nd row. These 10 rows form the pattern. Continue in pattern st until back measures 45 cm (17½ in) ending with the right side facing for next row. **Shape armholes:** by casting off 6 [7, 8] sts at beg. of the next 2 rows, then dec. 1 st at each end of next and every alt. row until 94 [98, 102] sts remain. Continue on these sts till back measures 67 [69, 69] cm

(26½ [27, 27] in) ending right side facing for next row. **Shape shoulders:** by casting off 15 [16, 16] sts at beg. of next 2 rows and 15 [16, 17] sts at beg. of the following 2 rows. **Cast off** remaining 34 [34, 36] sts.

Front
Work as for back until front measures 16 rows less than back to armhole shaping, ending with right side facing for next row. **Next row:** pattern 60 [63, 66] sts, turn and slip remaining sts on to a length of yarn. Now dec. 1 st at neck edge on 2nd and every following 4th row until front matches back at side edge up to armhole, ending at side edge. **Shape armhole:** (still dec. at neck edge as before on every 4th row from previous dec.) by casting off 6 [7, 8] sts at beg. of next row. Then dec. 1 st at armhole edge on every alt. row until 7 decreases *in all* have been worked at armhole edge. Continue dec. at neck edge only on every 4th row, as before, until 30 [32, 33] sts remain. Continue on these sts until front matches back at armhole edge up to shoulder, ending with right side facing for next row. **Shape shoulder:** by casting off 15 [16, 16] sts at beg. of next row. Work 1 row. Cast off remaining 15 [16, 17] sts. Rejoin yarn to remaining sts and complete to match first side reversing shapings.

Sleeves (2)
With 2½-mm needles cast on 56 [58, 60] sts and work in single rib for 23 rows. **Next row:** rib 5 [7, 4] sts, inc. in next st,

rib 4 [3, 3] sts, 9 [11, 13] times, inc. in next st, rib to end 66 [70, 74] sts. Change to 4½-mm needles and cable pattern as follows: **1st and 3rd rows:** k5 [6, 7], (p2, k8, p2, k10 [11, 12]) twice, p2, k8, p2, k5 [6, 7]. **2nd, 4th and 6th rows:** p5 [6, 7], (k2, p8, k2, p10 [11, 12]) twice, k2, p8, k2, p5 [6, 7]. **5th row:** as 1st row but working c4 in place of k8. **7th row:** inc. in 1st st; k4 [5, 6], (p2, k8, p2, k10 [11, 12]) twice, p2, k8, p2, k4 [5, 6], inc. in last st. **8th row:** p6 [7, 8], (k2, p8, k2, p10 [11, 12]) twice, k2, p8, k2, p6 [7, 8]. **9th row:** k6 [7, 8], (p2, k8, p2, k10 [11, 12]) twice, p2, k8, p2, k6 [7, 8]. **10th row:** as 8th. Continue in pattern, inc. 1 st at each end of 5th and every following 8th row until there are 90 [94, 98] sts – working extra sts in stocking st. Continue until sleeve measures 43 cm (19 in) from beg. **Shape top:** by casting off 6 [7, 8] sts at beg. of next 2 rows and then dec. 1 st at each end of the next and every alt. row until 44 [46, 46] sts remain. Work 1 row. Cast off 7 [6, 6] sts at beg. of next 4 [6, 6] rows. **Cast off.**

Neckband and making up
Join up right shoulder seam and then, with right side facing and 3-mm needles, starting at left shoulder pick up and knit 75 [78, 80] sts down left side of neck, 1 st by picking up loop that lies at centre 'V' and knitting through back (mark this st with a piece of coloured thread), 75 [78, 80] sts up right side of neck and 34 [34, 36] sts from cast-off sts on back neck 186 [192, 198] sts. Work 10 rows in single rib, dec. 1 st at each side of centre st on *every* row. **Cast off** *ribwise*. Sew up all seams carefully using overstitch or flatstitch.

Cross-Stitch Embroidery
gives Chic to this New
KNITTED JUMPER

*N*O, it isn't the least bit difficult! Glance at the simple charts below to see how quickly you'll do the "peasant" stitching

*S*UCH a charming jumper! Choose it in green or Coronation gold, with white stitching.

THE FRONT

With jade thread and No. 11 needles, commence at lower edge, casting on 126 sts. K. in rib of k. 1, p. 1, for 3 inches.
1st row (above ribbing)—P. 19, * p. 1 and k. 1 into next st., then k. 1 and p. 1 into next st., p. 8 *, rep. from * to * 3 times, p. 16, rep. from * to * 4 times, p. 11 (142 sts.).
2nd row—K. 20, * p. 2, k. 10 *, rep. from * to * twice, p. 2, k. 26, rep. from * to * 3 times, p. 2, k. 20. **3rd row**—P. 20, * k. 2, p. 10, rep. from * to * twice, k. 2, p. 26, rep. from * to * 3 times, k. 2, p. 20 Rep. last 2 rows 6 times. **16th row**—Inc., k. in patt. until 1 rem., inc. Next 15 rows—K. in patt. Rep. last 16 rows 3 times, then rep. 16th row (152 sts.). Next 9 rows—K. in patt. Now shape armholes. Next 2 rows—Cast off 7, k. in patt. to end. Next 4 rows—Cast off 3, k. in patt. to end (126 sts.).
Next 34 rows—K. in patt.
130th row—K. 11, * k. 2 tog., k. 2 tog., k. 8 *, rep. from * to * twice, k. 2 tog., k. 2 tog., k. 4, slip these sts. on to stitchholder, cast off 16 for neck, k. 4, rep. from * to * 3 times, k. 2 tog., k. 2 tog., k. 1†.
131st row—P. **132nd row**—K. 2 tog., k. to end. Rep. last 2 rows 14 times (32 sts.). **161st row**—P. **162nd row**—K. 24, turn; p. 24. **164th row**—K. 16 turn; p. 16.
166th row—K. 8, turn; p. 8. Cast off. Return to other shoulder, slip sts. from stitchholder to needle, point toward neck, join on thread. **131st row**—P. **132nd row**—K. until 2 rem., k. 2 tog. Rep. last 2 rows 14 times (32 sts.). **161st row**—P. 24, turn; k. 24. **163rd row**—P. 16, turn; k. 16. **165th row**—P. 8, turn; k. 8. Cast off.

THE BACK

With No. 11 needles, commence at lower edge, casting on 126 sts. K. in rib of k. 1, p. 1, for 3 inches. **Next row**—P. K. 88 rows st.-st. increasing 1 st. at beginning and end of 23rd, 45th and 67th rows (132 sts.). Now shape armholes. **90th row**—Cast off 7, k. to end. **91st row**—Cast off 7, p. to end. **92nd row**—Cast off 3, k. to end.
93rd row—Cast off 3, p. to end. Rep. last 2 rows once (106 sts.). K. 53 rows st.-st. Now shape shoulders. **149th row**—Cast off 8, p. to end. **150th row**—Cast off 8, k. to end. Rep. last 2 rows 3 times. Cast off.

THE RIGHT SLEEVE

With No. 11 needles commence at lower edge, casting on 78 sts. K. in rib of k. 1, p. 1, for 14 rows. **15th row**—K. 3, * k. 1, inc. *, rep. from * to * 9 times, inc., inc., k. 8, inc., inc., k. 10, inc., inc., k. 8, inc., inc., rep. from * to * 9 times, inc., inc., k. 2 (106 sts.). **16th row**—P. 34, k. 2, p. 9, k. 2, p. 12 k. 2, p. 9, k. 2, p. 34. **17th row**—K. 34, p. 2, k. 9, p. 2, k. 12, p. 2, k. 9, p. 2, k. 34. Rep. last 2 rows 3 times. **24th row**—As 16th row. **25th row**—Inc., k. in patt. until 1 rem., inc. **Next 9 rows**—K. in patt.

(Please turn to page xxvi)

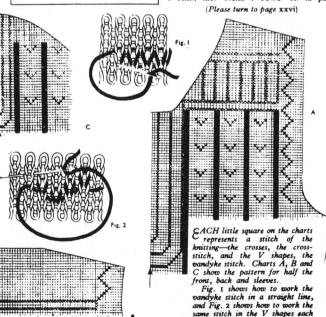

Fig. 1

Fig. 2

*E*ACH little square on the charts represents a stitch of the knitting—the crosses, the cross-stitch, and the V shapes, the vandyke stitch. Charts A, B and C show the pattern for half the front, back and sleeves.
Fig. 1 shows how to work the vandyke stitch in a straight line, and Fig. 2 shows how to work the same stitch in the V shapes each side of centre-front and sleeves.

KNITTING

Twin set: cardigan and short-sleeved jumper

(This consists of a cardigan and matching short-sleeved jumper)

Measurements Bust: 85 [90] cm (33½ [35½] in). Length: 52 [53] cm (20½ [21] in). Sleeve seam: 45 cm (17½ in)

Materials Cardigan: 16 × 25 gm balls of 4-ply yarn, 8 buttons to match. Jumper: 9 × 25 gm balls of 4-ply yarn, 3 small buttons to match

Needles A pair each of 2½-mm (No. 12), 3½-mm (No. 9) and 4-mm (No. 8) and also a medium-size crochet hook

Abbreviations See page 16

Tension 12 sts of zigzag pattern equal 5 cm (2 in) on 4-mm needles

Cardigan

Back

With 2½-mm needles cast on 104 [120] sts and work in single rib for 8 [9] cm (3 [3½] in) inc. 10 sts evenly along last row (114 [130] sts). Change to 4-mm needles and work pattern as follows: **1st row:** sl1, *k2 tog., k5, inc. in each of next 2 sts, k5, k2 tog., rep. from * to last st, k1 tbl. **2nd row:** purl. Rep. last 2 rows 3 times more then rep. 1st row again. **10th row:** all knit – on the wrong side so this makes the ridge running between motifs on right side. These 10 rows form zigzag pattern. Rep. 10 pattern rows twice more then change to 3½-mm needles and work in stocking st, inc. at each end of next and every following 6th row till there are 124 [138] sts on needle. Then carry on without shaping till work is 34[35] cm (13½ [14]in).

Shape armholes: cast off 6 sts at beg. of next 2 rows then dec. 1 st at each end of every row until 106 [118] sts remain. Work 8 cm (3 in) more in stocking st and then work 10 cm (4 in) in lacy st. **1st row:** knit. **2nd row:** sl1, * p3, k3, rep. from * to last st, k1 tbl. **3rd row:** sl1, *k1, wl.fwd, k2 tog., k3, rep. from * to last st, k1 tbl. **4th row:** as 2nd. **5th row:** knit. **6th row:** as 2nd. **7th row:** sl1, * k2 tog., wl.fwd, k1 k3, rep. from * to last st, k1 tbl. **8th row:** as 2nd. These 8 rows form the pattern. **Shape shoulders:** in stocking st cast off 16 sts at beg of next 4 rows. Leave the remaining sts on a safety-pin for neckband.

Right front and band

With 2½-mm needles cast on 64 [80] sts and work in single rib (always starting rows with a slip st) for 4 rows. Make a buttonhole as follows: **1st row:** rib 5, cast off 4 sts, rib to end. **2nd row:** rib to last 9 sts, cast on 4 sts, rib 5. Work another 22 rows in single rib and then make another buttonhole as above. Continue in rib till work measures 9 cm (3½ in) from start, leaving 14 sts for front band on a safety-pin. Change to 4-mm needles and work 3 motifs. Change to 3½-mm needles and now work in stocking st, inc. at side edge only on next and every following 6th row until there are 62 [78] sts on needle. Work without further shaping until work measures 34 [36] in (13½ [14] in) ending at side edge. **Shape armhole:** cast off 6 sts at beg. of next row and then dec. 1 st at armhole edge on *every* row till there are

50 [62] sts on needle. Work straight in stocking st until work measures same as back to start of lacy pattern. Work in lace st for about 4 cm (1½ in), finishing at neck edge. **Shape neck**: by casting off 10 sts at beg. of next row and then dec. 1 st on *every* row at neck edge until 32 sts remain, keeping lacy pattern throughout. Then continue straight until work measures same as back to shoulder, finishing at shoulder edge. **Shape shoulders**: by casting off 16 sts at beg. of next row and following alt. row. **Right front band**: Rejoin yarn to 14 sts left on safety-pin and with 2½-mm needles continue rib, making buttonholes as before with 22 rows in between each. Work until 50 [51] cm (19½ [20] in) long – this should fit up front *very slightly stretched*. Leave sts on safety-pin to pick up for neckband.

Left front and band
Work as for right front and band reversing all shapings and omitting buttonholes.

Sleeves (2)
Using 2½-mm needles cast on 50 sts and work in single rib for 9 cm (3½ in) finishing with wrong side facing. **Next row**: rib 17, inc. in each of next 16 sts, rib 17. Change to 4-mm needles and work 3 motifs as on back. Then change to 3½-mm needles and work in stocking st inc. at each end of next and every following 6th row until 108 [112] sts are on the needle. Then continue straight until work measures 45 cm (17½ in) from start. **Shape top**: by casting off 1 st at beg. of next 10 rows, then 2 sts at beg. of every row till 24 sts remain. **Cast off** *loosely* knitting 2 sts tog. as you cast off, *all* along row.

Neckband
With 2½-mm needles and right side of work facing pick up 14 sts from right front band, 25 sts up right side of neck, sts left from back neck, 25 sts down left side of neck and 14 sts from left front band. Work 8 rows in single rib, making final buttonhole in right band on 4th and

5th rows of rib. **Cast off** *ribwise*, loosely (looseness easily achieved holding a larger needle – say 3¼-mm – in right hand).

Making up
Sew up carefully using flatstitch or overstitch. Attach buttons to correspond with buttonholes.

Short-sleeved jumper

Back
Work as for back of cardigan until 3 patterns have been worked. Then carry on in same pattern – *not changing stocking st* – until work is 33 [34] cm (13 [13½] in) from start – 8 patterns (of 10 rows each) after rib. **Shape armholes**: by casting off 10 sts at start of next 2 rows

and then dec. 1 st at each end of *every* row until 98 sts are on needle. Carry on straight in pattern until 6 patterns have been worked from armhole start. **Shape shoulders:** by casting off 16 sts at start of next 4 rows. Leave remaining sts on a safety-pin to pick up for neckband.

Front
Work as for back until 4 motifs have been worked from armhole. **Shape neck:** work across 34 sts, turn (leaving remaining sts on spare needle). Work 2 complete patterns. **Shape shoulders:** by casting off 17 sts at beg. of next and following alt. row, working last 2 sts tog. on each cast-off st. Slip middle 30 sts on to a safety-pin or piece of thread to pick up for the neckband. Rejoin yarn to last 34 sts and work to match first side, reversing shapings.

Sleeves (2)
Starting at the top. Using 4-mm needles cast on 17 sts and purl 1 row, inc. in every stitch on next row (34) sts. Purl 1 row. Commence in pattern as follows: **1st row:** as 1st row on pattern for back. **2nd row:** k1 and p1 in 1st st, purl to last st, k1 and p1 into this last st. **3rd row:** sl1, k1, then rep. from * in 1st row, to last 2 sts, k2. **4th row:** as 2nd. **5th row:** sl1, k2, then rep. from * in 1st row, to last 3 sts, k3. **6th row:** as 2nd. **7th row:** sl1, k3, rep. from * in 1st row, to last 4 sts, k4.

8th row: as 2nd. **9th row:** sl1, k4, repeat from * in 1st row to last 5 sts, k5. **10th row:** all knit (44 sts). Continue working in this way inc. 1 st at both ends of every wrong side row until there are 16 sts extra at each end. Then the 1st row will read exactly as 1st pattern row on back. Inc. on the next wrong side row as before and continue as on inc. pattern above until there are 82 sts altogether. There will now be a half pattern at beg. and end of row but as the pattern is so clearly seen now there will be no difficulty in keeping this correct. Now continue straight, working from 3rd row of pattern till 1½ patterns have been worked on the straight. Work 13 rows of single rib on 2½-mm needles. **Cast off** loosely.

Neckband
Using 2½-mm needles with right side facing and starting at left shoulder pick up 25 sts down left front, the 30 sts from centre front, 25 sts up right front and sts left from back. Work 8 rows in single rib. **Cast off** *ribwise*, loosely (looseness easily achieved by holding a 3¼-mm needle in right hand).

Making up
Sew up carefully, leaving left shoulder open for 9 cm (3½ in). Neatly double crochet or blanket st opening. Make 3 loop buttonholes and then attach buttons to correspond.

KNITTING

Double-knit cardigan with Jacquard yoke

Measurements Bust: 84 [89] cm
(33 [35] in)
Materials 13 × 25 gm balls of double-knitting yarn in main colour (M) and 1
ball of each contrast (O, X, Y, B, H, K)
Needles A pair each of 4-mm (No. 8)
and 5-mm (No. 6) and 7 buttons to match
Abbreviations See page 16
Tension 9 sts equal 5 cm (2 in) on 5-mm
needles in stocking st

Back

Using 4-mm needles and main colour cast
on 80 [90] sts and work in single rib for
9 cm (3½ in). Change to 5-mm needles and
work in stocking st until work measures
32 [33] cm (12½ [13] in). **Shape armhole:**
casting off 3 sts at beg. of next 2 rows and
2 sts at beg. of the following 2 rows
(70 [80] sts). Now work Fair Isle yoke as
follows: **1st row:** k in O. **2nd row:** p in
X. **3rd row:** *k1X, k2Y, k2X, k2Y, k3X
rep. from * to end. **4th row:** *p2X, p2Y,
p2X, p2Y, p2X rep. from * to end. **5th
row:** *k1X, k4Y, k2X, k2Y, k1X rep. from
* to end. **6th row:** *p2Y, p2X, p2Y, p2X,
p2Y rep. from * to end. **7th row:** *k1X,
k2Y, k2X, k4Y, k1X rep. from * to end.
8th row: p in X. **9th row:** k in O. **10th
row:** p in B. **11th row:** *k2B, k2O rep.
from * to last 2 sts, k2B. **12th row:** (*small
size*) p2B *p2O, p2B rep. from * to end.
(*other size*) *p2O, p2B rep. from * to end.
13th row: k in B. **14th row:** p in O. **15th
row:** k in H. **16th row:** p in H. **17th row:**
*k5K, k5H, rep. from * to end. **18th row:**
*p4H, p2K, p3H, p1K, rep. from * to
end. **19th row:** *k1K, k1H, k1K, k1H,
k3K, k3H rep from * to end. **20th row:**
*p2H, p2K, p1H, p1K, p1H, p3K rep.
from * to end. **21st row:** *k4H, k1K,
k2H, k2K, k1H rep. from * to end.
22nd row: *p2K, p3H, p1K, p4H
rep. from * to end. **23rd row:** *k1K,
k3H, k1K, k4H, k1K rep. from
* to end. **24th row:** *p1H, p1K, p3H,
p1K, p2H, p2K rep. from * to end. **25th
row:** *k1H, k2K, k1H, k1K, k3H, k1K,
k1H rep. from * to end. **26th row:** *p1H,
p1K, p3H, p3K, p2H rep. from * to end.
27th row: *k4H, k5K, k1H rep. from * to
end. **28th row:** p in H. **29th row:** k in O.
30th row: p in B. **31st row:** as 11th.
32nd row: as 12th. **33rd row:** k in B.
34th row: p in O. **35th row:** k in M.
36th row: p in M. **37th row:** as 35th.
38th row: as 36th. **Shape shoulders:** by
casting off 11 [15] sts at start of the next 4
rows (*armhole edge*) **Cast off** remaining sts.

Fronts (2)

Using 4-mm needles and main colour cast
on 35 [45] sts and work in single rib for
9 cm (3½ in). Change to 5-mm needles and
work in stocking st until work measures
32 [33] cm (12½ [13] in) finishing at side
(*armhole edge*). **Shape armhole:** by
casting off 3 sts at start of next row and 2
sts at start of next alt. row (*next row
starting at armhole edge*). Now knit 1 or 2
rows in stocking st so that you can start
Fair Isle pattern with *right* side of work
facing. Next work Fair Isle yoke as on
back until you have worked row 28 (29 on
second front) ending at neck (*front*) edge.
Shape neck: *at the same time continuing*

pattern by casting off 2 sts at start of next row, then dec. 1 st at this (neck) edge on every row until 22 [30] sts remain, working in main colour once pattern is finished and making sure front armhole measures same as back. Finish at armhole edge.

Shape shoulders: by casting off 11 [15] sts on next and following alt. row. *Make sure second front has all shapings reversed.*

Sleeves (2)

All worked in plain main colour. Using 4-mm needles cast on 39 sts and work in single rib for 9 cm (3½ in), inc. 1 st at each end of last row. Change to 5-mm needles and work in stocking st, inc. 1 st at each end of the 5th and every following 6th row until there are 65 [69]

sts on needle then work straight until sleeve measures 43 cms (17 in) from start. **Shape top of sleeve:** by casting off 3 sts at beg. of next 4 rows and then dec. 1 st at both ends of every alt. row until 23 sts remain, then *every* row till 15 sts remain. **Cast off.**

Right front band

Using 4-mm needles and main colour cast on 7 sts and work in garter st for 1½ cm (½ in). Make buttonhole in next row by k3, wl.fwd, k2 tog., k2. Continue in garter st making a buttonhole at intervals of 8 cm (3 in) until 6 buttonholes have been worked (with 1st buttonhole coming after 1½ cm (½ in) and the next five 8 cm (3 in) apart). Band should on the 6th buttonhole measure 39 cm (15½ in). **Cast off.**

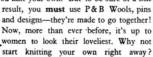

Left front band

Work in garter st until same length as right band. **Cast off.**

Neckband

Using 4-mm needles and main colour cast on 84 sts and work in garter st for 6 rows. **Next row:** k3, wl.fwd, k2 tog., k to end of row. k4 more rows. **Cast off** *knitwise* and not too tightly.

Making up

Join side, sleeve and shoulder seams using overstitch or flatstitch. Set sleeves into armholes. Stitch right front band to right front and left band to left front, making sure the bands fit fronts with fronts lying flat and straight, also that when buttons are attached front bands are exactly the same size. Stitch neckband to edge of neck. Attach buttons to left front to correspond with buttonholes.

Some suggested colour combinations

M: red   M: grey
O: navy   O: black
X: emerald   X: cream
Y: pink   Y: rust
B: gold   B: gold
H: pale blue   H: rust
K: royal blue   K: cream

M: burgundy   M: camel
O: black   O: black
X: oyster (pinky beige)   X: grey
Y: pilot blue   Y: gold
B: dusty pink   B: cream
H: airforce blue (greyish blue)   H: rust
K: burgundy   K: gold

M: pilot blue
O: black
X: grey
Y: cream
B: pale blue
H: burgundy
K: cream

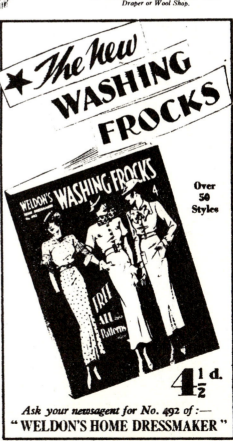

KNITTING

Old-fashioned 4-ply cardigan

Measurements Bust: 89 cm (35 in).
Length: 50 cm (19½ in). Sleeve seam:
43 cm (17 in)
Materials 10 × 20 gm balls of 4-ply
wool or similar weight yarn, 1 × 20 gm
ball in contrast colour and 8 buttons to
match
Needles A pair each of 3-mm (No. 11)
and 3½-mm (No. 9)
Abbreviations See page 16
Tension 18 rows and 14 sts equal a
square of 5 cm (2 in) using 3½-mm needles

Back

Using 3-mm needles and main colour cast
on 104 sts and work 9 cm (3½ in) in single
rib. Change to 3½-mm needles and
2-colour pattern as follows: **1st row:** knit
main colour. **2nd row:** purl in main
colour. **3rd row:** sl1, k2 main *k1
contrast colour, k5 main and repeat from *
to last 3 sts, k1 contrast, k2 main. Work 5
rows in stocking st in main colour,
increasing at each end of the 4th row. **9th
row:** sl1, k5 main *k1 contrast, k5
main, rep. from * to end. Then work 5
more rows in stocking st. This completes
the pattern rows 3rd to 14th. Repeat from
the 3rd to 14th, *at the same time increasing
at each end of every* 6th row until there are
118 sts on the needle. Then work straight
until work measures 32 cm (12½ in).
Shape armholes: by casting off 7 sts at
the start of the next 2 rows. Then
decrease 1 st at both ends of every row
until there are 96 sts on the needle, all the
time continuing in the 2-colour pattern,
and finishing at the end of a purl row.

Now with the right side facing start
working the Fair Isle yoke from chart (32
rows). Next work in stocking st in main
colour only until work measures 48 cm
(19 in) from beg. **Shape shoulders:** by
casting off 7 sts at the beg. of the next 8
rows. **Cast off.**

Fronts (2)

Using 3-mm needles and main colour cast
on 48 sts and work in single rib for 9 cm
(3 in). Change to 3½-mm needles and
2-colour pattern as for back increasing at
beg. of the 4th and every following 6th
row until 56 sts are on the needle. Work
straight until work is 32 cm (12½ in)
finishing at side (shaped) edge. **Shape
armholes:** continuing in pattern cast off
7 sts at the beg. of the next row. Then
dec. 1 st at this same edge on every
row until there are 42 sts on the needle,
finishing with the right side facing. Now
work Fair Isle yoke following the chart.
Work 20 rows of chart then at the start of
the next row – which should be the *front
edge* shape for the neck – making sure to
keep the Fair Isle pattern correct, cast off
2 sts. Continue to dec. 1 st at this same
edge on *every* row until 28 sts remain.
Work without further shaping until work
measures 48 cm (19 in) from beg. (same as
back) ending at armhole edge. (N.B. you
will find this is only 1 or 2 rows after
finishing the chart after which main colour
alone is used.) **Shape shoulders:** by
casting off 7 sts at the beg. of next row.
Work 1 row plain. Repeat the last 2 rows

twice more then cast off remaining sts. *Remember to reverse all shapings on second front.*

Sleeves (2)

Using 3-mm needles and main colour (the

sleeves are in plain main colour) cast on 48 sts and work in single rib for 8 cm (3 in) inc. to 56 sts evenly on the last row of rib. Change to $3\frac{1}{2}$-mm needles and work in plain stocking st, inc. at each end of the 4th and every following 6th row until there are 76 sts on the needle. Continue without further shaping until work measures 43 cm (17 in) from start. **Shape top of sleeve:** by dec. 1 st at both ends of every alternate row until there are 40 sts on the needle. Then dec. 1 st at both ends of every row until there are 20 sts. **Cast off.**

Right front band

Using 3-mm needles cast on 9 sts and work in garter st for $1\frac{1}{2}$ cm ($\frac{1}{2}$ in). Make buttonhole in the next 2 rows as follows: k3, cast off 3, k3. **Next row:** k3, cast on 3, k3. Continue in garter st making a further 6 buttonholes at intervals of 6 cm ($2\frac{1}{2}$ in) measured from the *cast-off* edge of the previous buttonhole. **Cast off** when the band measures 39 cm ($15\frac{1}{2}$ in) from the beginning.

Left front band

Work as for right front band omitting buttonholes.

Neckband

Using 3-mm needles cast on 104 sts and work in garter st for $1\frac{1}{2}$ cm ($\frac{1}{2}$ in). Make a buttonhole in the next 2 rows thus: **Next row:** k3, cast off 3, work to the end of row. **Next row:** knit to the edge of the cast-off sts, cast on 3, k3. Continue in garter st until work measures $2\frac{1}{2}$ cm (1 in). **Cast off** *loosely*. (The easiest way to do this is to cast off with a $3\frac{1}{2}$-mm needle.)

Making up

Using overstitch or flatstitch join side, sleeve and shoulder seams and set sleeves into the armholes. Stitch right front band to right front and left band to left front. Stitch the neckband to the edge of the neck. Attach buttons to left front band to correspond with buttonholes. *Do not press,*

but firmly smooth with hands and fold.
See page 16 for washing instructions.

Some suggested colour combinations

main colour either:

navy
or airforce blue
(greyish blue) } with cream
or camel as contrast
or grey

main colour either:
burgundy
or mink
or bottle green } with white
or red as contrast
or bright blue

main colour: cream   contrast: rust
main colour: white   contrast: red
main colour natural   contrast: mid brown

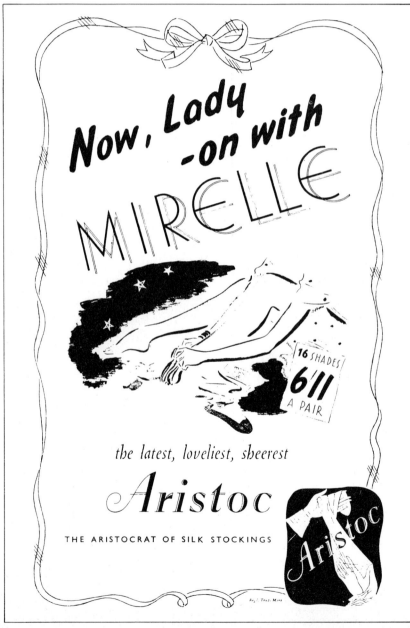
Fair Isle chart

o	o	o	o	o	o	32
o	o	x	o	o	o	31
o	x	o	x	o	o	30
x	o	x	o	x	o	29
o	x	o	x	o	x	28
x	o	o	o	x	o	27
o	x	o	x	o	o	26
o	o	x	o	o	o	25
o	o	o	o	o	o	24
o	o	o	o	o	o	23
o	o	x	o	o	x	22
x	o	x	o	x	o	21
x	o	x	o	x	x	20
x	o	x	o	x	x	19
x	o	x	o	x	x	18
o	o	x	o	o	x	17
x	o	x	o	x	o	16
x	o	x	o	x	x	15
x	o	x	o	x	x	14
x	o	x	o	x	x	13
o	o	x	o	o	x	12
x	o	x	o	x	o	11
x	o	x	o	x	o	10
x	o	x	o	x	x	9
x	o	x	o	x	x	8
o	x	o	x	o	x	7
o	o	o	o	o	o	6
o	o	o	o	o	o	5
o	o	x	o	o	o	4
o	x	x	x	o	o	3
x	x	x	x	x	o	2
x	x	x	x	x	x	1

6 stitch repeat

o: main colour

x: contrast

KNITTING

Knot and bobble cardigan

Measurements Bust: 89 cm (35 in).
Length: 57 cm (22½ in). Sleeve seam:
45 cm (17½ in)
Materials 12 × 25 gm balls of 4-ply
yarn and 7 buttons to match
Needles A pair each of 2½-mm (No. 12)
and 4-mm (No. 8) plus a medium-size
crochet hook
Abbreviations See page 16
Tension 12 sts equal 5 cm (2 in) on
4-mm needles

Note
To make knot (mk) p3 tog., leave sts on
left-hand needle, wrn, then purl into same
3 sts.
To make woolly ball or bobble (mb) p1, k1,
p1, k1, p1, into st thus making 5 sts out of
this st, turn k5, turn p5, sl 2nd, 3rd, 4th
and 5th sts over 1st st, push bobble to
front.

Back
Using 2½-mm needles cast on 104 sts and
work 9 cm (3½ in) in single rib. Change to
4-mm needles and work pattern as follows
(*wrong side facing*): **1st and every alt.
row:** purl. **2nd row:** knit. **4th row:** *k5,
mk, rep from * to end. **6th row:** knit. **8th
row:** k1, *mk, k5, rep. from * to last 7 sts,
mk, k4. These 8 rows form the pattern.
Work in pattern until back measures 38 cm
(15 in). from cast-on edge. **Shape
armhole:** *keeping pattern correct
throughout* cast off 7 sts at beg. of the next
2 rows, then k2 tog., at each end of the
next 9 rows. Continue straight until work
measures 57 cm (22½ in) from start.

Shape shoulder: cast off 8 sts at beg. of
next 6 rows leaving the remaining sts on a
spare needle.

Right front
Using 2½-mm needles cast on 56 sts and
work 9 cm (3½ in) in single rib. Change to
4-mm needles and work pattern as follows
(*wrong side facing*): **1st row and every
alt. row:** purl. **2nd row:** k23, p1, k to end.
4th row: k5, mb, k10, mb, k6, p1, *k5,
mk, rep. from * to end. **6th row:** as 2nd.
8th row: k9, mb, k10, mb, k2, p1, k1,
*mk, k5, rep. from * to last 7 sts, mk, k4.
10th row: as 2nd. **12th row:** k23, p1, *k5,
mk, rep. from * to end. **14th row:** k2,
mb, k10, mb, k8, mb, p1, k to end. **16th
row:** k23, p1, k1, *mk, k5, rep. from * to
last 7 sts, mk, k4. **18th row:** k7, mb, k9,
mb, k5, p1, k to end. **20th row:** k10, mb,
k12, p1, * k5, mk, rep. from * to end.
22nd row: as 2nd. **24th row:** k3, mb, k9,
mb, k6, mb, k2, p1, k1, *mk, k5, rep.
from * to last 7 sts, mk, k4. **26th row:** as
2nd. **28th row:** k10, mb, k12, p1, *k5,
mk, rep. from * to end. **30th row:** as 2nd.
32nd row: k1, mb, k16, mb, k4, p1, k1,
*mk, k5, rep. from * to last 7 sts, mk, k4.
These 32 rows form the pattern. Continue
in pattern st until front measures 38 cm
(15 in) from cast-on edge (*measure over
knot stitch part as this is flat*), ending at
armhole edge. **Shape armhole:** *keeping
pattern correct throughout* cast off 7 sts at
beg. of next row, then k2 tog. at armhole
edge on each of the next 7 rows. Continue
straight until work measures 51 cm (20 in)
from cast-on edge, finishing at front edge.

Shape neck: cast off 7 sts at beg. of next row, then dec. 1 st at front edge on *every* row until 24 sts remain. Work in pattern without shaping until front measures same as back to shoulder shaping. **Shape shoulder:** (*armhole edge*) cast off 8 sts at beg. of next and following 2 alt. rows.

Left front

Work as for right front, reversing all shapings and working 32 pattern rows in reverse, i.e. **2nd row:** k32, p1, k to end. **4th row:** *mk, k5, rep. from * 3 times more (32 sts), p1, k6, mb, k10, mb, k5. Work pattern from right to left *not* left to right – this is quite easy to do after working right front.

Sleeves (2)

Using 2½-mm needles cast on 39 sts and work 9 cm (3½ in) in single rib inc. on last rib row evenly to 64 sts. Change to 4-mm needles and pattern as on back inc. 1 st at each end of every 8th row until 80 sts are on the needle. Continue without further shaping until sleeve is 48 cm (19 in) from cast-on edge. **Shape top:** *keeping the pattern correct throughout* cast off 7 sts at beg. of next 2 rows, then k2 tog. at each end of *every* row until 38 sts remain, then at each end of every alt. row until 18 sts remain, ending right side row. **Cast off.**

Front bands (2)

Using 2½-mm needles cast on 9 sts and work in single rib until band fits up front *slightly stretched*, leaving sts on a safety-pin for neckband. **Buttonhole band:** work to match other band but insert buttonholes commencing on 5th row and then at 8 cm (3 in) intervals until 7 in all have been worked (last buttonhole should come 3 rows before end of band). **Buttonhole rows:** rib 3, cast off 2 sts, rib to end. **Next row:** rib to cast-off sts, cast on 2 sts, rib to end.

Neckband

With right side of work facing and 2½-mm needles pick up 104 sts evenly round neck including front bands. Work 2 rows in single rib and then a row of holes thus: *rib 2, k2 tog., yrn, rep. from * to last 4 sts, rib to end. Work 4 more rows in single rib. **Cast off** *ribwise*.

Making up

Join shoulder seams, pin and stitch sleeves into armholes, sew sleeve and side seams. Attach front bands and buttons to correspond with buttonholes. Crochet a cord approximately 127 cm (50 in) long and thread through small holes in neckband. Then make 2 small tassels and attach to each end of the neckband cord.

COMFORT and chic go hand in hand in a pretty style that trimly fits the average figure

In RIBBING and LACE Stitch...

A magyar jumper with the new muffler neck... asking to be knitted for your autumn wardrobe.

MATERIALS REQUIRED

9 oz. Sirdar crochet wool; 2 No. 11 Abel Morrall's '' Aero '' knitting needles; 2 No. 9 Abel Morrall's '' Aero '' knitting needles; 4 small buttons; medium-sized crochet hook.
To obtain the best results, use the exact materials mentioned above.

MEASUREMENTS

Round jumper, below arm-holes, 36 inches; shoulder to lower edge, 18 inches; sleeve seam, 21 inches (including cuff).

ABBREVIATIONS

K., knit; p., purl; st., stitch; tog., together; m., make; d.c., double crochet.
Tension of knitting on No. 9 needles about 7 stitches and 9 rows to 1 inch.
Always knit into back of cast-on stitches.

Front

USING No. 11 needles, cast on 120 sts. and work in ribbing of k. 1, p. 1 for 3½ inches.
Next row—P. 10, * p. twice into next st., p. 9, repeat from * to end of row. (131 sts.)
Change to No. 9 needles and work in pattern as follows:
1st row—* K. 5, m. 1, k. 2 tog., k. 1, m. 1, k. 2 tog., repeat from * till 1 st. remains, k. 1.
2nd and every alternate row—Purl.
3rd row—K. 6, * m. 1, k. 2 tog., k. 8, repeat from * till 5 sts. remain, m. 1, k. 2 tog., k. 3.
5th row—Knit. 7th row—K. 9, * m. 1, k. 2 tog., k. 1, m. 1, k. 2 tog., k. 5, repeat from * till 2 sts. remain, k. 2.
9th row—K. 10 * m. 1, k. 2 tog., k. 8, repeat from * till 1 st. remains, k. 1.
11th row—Knit. 12th row—Purl.
Repeat these 12 rows 6 more times.
Now shape for armholes.
1st row—Cast off 3, k. 2, m. 1, k. 2 tog., k. 1, m. 1, k. 2 tog., repeat from * in 1st pattern row till 1 st. remains, k. 1.
2nd row—Cast off 3, p. to end of row.
3rd row—K. 2 tog., k. 1, * m. 1, k. 2 tog., k. 8, repeat from * till 2 sts. remain, k. 2 tog.
4th and every alternate row—P. 2 tog., p. till 2 sts. remain, p. 2 tog.
5th row—K. 2 tog., k. till 2 sts. remain, k. 2 tog. 7th row—K. 2 tog., * m. 1, k. 2 tog., k. 1, m. 1, k. 2 tog., k. 5, repeat from * till 5 sts. remain, m. 1, k. 2 tog., k. 2 tog. 9th row—K. 2 tog., k. 9, * m. 1, k. 2 tog., k. 8, repeat from * till 2 sts. remain, k. 2 tog. 11th row—As 5th row. 13th row—K. 2 tog., * m. 1, k. 2 tog., k. 1, m. 1, k. 2 tog., k. 5, repeat from * till 3 sts. remain, k. 1, k. 2 tog.
15th row—K. 2 tog., k. 9, * m. 1, k. 2 tog., k. 8, repeat from * till 10 sts. remain, m. 1, k. 2 tog., k. 6, k. 2 tog.
17th row—As 5th row.
19th row—K. 2 tog., * k. 1, m. 1, k. 2 tog., k. 5, m. 1, k. 2 tog., repeat from * till 11 sts. remain, k. 1, m. 1, k. 2 tog., k. 6, k. 2 tog. 21st row—K. 2 tog., k. 7, * m. 1, k. 2 tog., k. 8, repeat from * till 10 sts. remain, m. 1, k. 2 tog., k. 6, k. 2 tog. 23rd row—As 5th row.
25th row—K. 2 tog., * k. 1, m. 1, k. 2 tog., k. 5, m. 1, k. 2 tog., repeat from * till 9 sts. remain, k. 1, m. 1, k. 2 tog., k. 4, k. 2 tog. 27th row—K. 2 tog., k. 7, * m. 1, k. 2 tog., k. 8, repeat from * till 8 sts. remain, k. 1, k. 2 tog., k. 4, k. 2 tog.
29th row—As 5th row.
31st row—K. 2 tog., k. 1, * k. 5, m. 1, k. 2 tog., k. 1, m. 1, k. 2 tog., repeat from * till 6 sts. remain, k. 4, k. 2 tog.
33rd row—K. 2 tog., k. 5, * m. 1, k. 2 tog., k. 8, repeat from * till 8 sts. remain, m. 1, k. 2 tog., k. 4, k. 2 tog.
35th row—As 5th row.
37th row—K. 2 tog., k. 1, * k. 5, m. 1, k. 2 tog., k. 1, m. 1, k. 2 tog., repeat from * till 4 sts. remain, k. 2, k. 2 tog.
39th row—K. 2 tog., k. 5, * m. 1, k. 2 tog., k. 8, repeat from * till 6 sts. remain, m. 1, k. 2 tog., k. 2, k. 2 tog.
41st row—As 5th row.
43rd row—K. 2 tog., k. 4, * m. 1, k. 2 tog., k. 1, m. 1, k. 2 tog., k. 5, repeat from * till 9 sts. remain, m. 1, k. 2 tog., k. 1, m. 1, k. 2 tog., k. 2, k. 2 tog.
45th row—K. 2 tog., k. 3, * m. 1, k. 2 tog., k. 8, repeat from * till 6 sts. remain, m. 1, k. 2 tog., k. 2, k. 2 tog.
46th row—As 4th row. (37 sts.)
47th row—Knit. 48th row—Purl. Cast off.

Back

Work exactly as for front until 28th row of armhole shaping has been completed. (73 sts.) Now work as follows:
1st row—K. 2 tog., k. 34, turn. Put the remaining 37 sts. on a spare needle.
2nd and every alternate row—P. till 2 sts. remain, p. 2 tog. 3rd row—K. 2 tog., k. 1 (k. 5, m. 1, k. 2 tog., k. 1, m. 1, k. 2 tog.) 3 times, k. 1. 5th row—K. 2 tog., k. 5 (m. 1, k. 2 tog., k. 8) twice, m. 1, k. 2 tog., k. 3. 7th row—K. 2 tog., k. to end of row. 9th row—K. 2 tog., k. 1 (k. 5, m. 1, k. 2 tog., k. 1, m. 1, k. 2 tog.) twice. k. 5. 11th row—K. 2 tog., k: 5,
(*Please turn to page 115*)

SHOWING that the button-fastened back is as smart as the front and the lace stitch as easy as it is fascinating.

NOTE: In these instructions the stitch remaining on right hand needle after cast off is included in instructions stated immediately after.

Reminder: Eileen Maxwell is always delighted to help you with knitting or craft problems. See Coupon on page 100.

Fashion's Star Turn...

Front

CAST on 74 sts. on No. 10 needles and work in pattern as follows :

1st row—S. 1, * k. 1, m. 1, k. 3, k. 2 tog., rep. from * till 1 st. remains, k. 1.

2nd and every alternate row—Purl.

3rd row—S. 1, * k. 2, m. 1, k. 2, k. 2 tog., rep. from * till 1 st. remain, k. 1.

5th row—S. 1, * k. 3, m. 1, k. 3 tog., m. 1, rep. from * till 1 st. remains, k. 1.

7th row—S. 1, * m. 1, k. 3, k. 2 tog., k. 1, rep. from * till 1 st. remains, k. 1. Change to No. 5 needles. **9th row**—S. 1, * k. 1, m. 1, k. 2, k. 2 tog., k. 1, rep. from * till 1 st. remains, k. 1. **11th row**—S. 1, k. 2, * m. 1, k. 3 tog., m. 1, k. 3, rep. from * till 5 sts. remain, m. 1, k. 3 tog., m. 1, k. 2. **13th row**—S. 1, k. 2, * k. 2 tog., k. 1, m. 1, k. 3, rep. from * till 5 sts. remain, k. 2 tog., k. 1, m. 1, k. 2.

15th row—S. 1, k. 1, k. 2 tog., * k. 2, m. 1, k. 2, k. 2 tog., rep. from * till 4 sts. remain, k. 2, m. 1, k. 2.

17th row—K. 2 tog., * m. 1, k. 3, m. 1, k. 3 tog., rep. from * till 6 sts. remain, m. 1, k. 3, m. 1, k. 2 tog., k. 1.

18th row—Purl. These 18 rows form the pattern.

Rep. pattern twice. Now shape for armholes. **1st row**—Cast off 6, s. 1, * k. 1, m. 1, k. 3, k. 2 tog., rep. from * till 1 st. remains, k. 1. **2nd row**—Cast off 6, p. to end of row (62 sts.).

3rd row—As 3rd pattern row.

4th row—Purl. **5th row**—As 5th pattern row. **6th row**—Purl.

7th row—As 7th pattern row.

8th row—Purl. **9th row**—S. 1, (k. 1, m. 1, k. 2, k. 2 tog., k. 1) 4 times, k. 1, m. 1, k. 2, k. 2 tog., inc., inc., m. 1, k. 2, k. 2 tog., k. 1, (k. 1, m. 1, k. 2, k. 2 tog., k. 1) 4 times, k. 1. **10th row**—Purl.

11th row—S. 1, k. 2, (m. 1, k. 3 tog., m. 1, k. 3) 5 times, (k. 2, m. 1, k. 3 tog., m. 1, k. 3) 5 times, k. 1. **12th row**—P. 31, inc., inc., p. 31. **13th row**—S. 1, k. 2, (k. 2 tog., k. 1, m, 1, k. 3) 5 times, k. 1, (k. 3, k. 2 tog., k. 1, m. 1) 5 times, k. 2. **14th row**—Purl. **15th row**—S. 1, k. 1, (k. 2 tog., k. 2, m. 1, k. 2) 5 times, inc., inc., (k. 2, k. 2 tog., k. 2, m. 1) 5 times, k. 2. **16th row**—Purl.

17th row—As 17th pattern row.

18th row—K. 33, inc., inc., k. 33.

19th row—S. 1, (k. 1, m. 1, k. 3, k. 2 tog.) 6 times, k. 2, (k. 1, m. 1, k. 3, k. 2 tog.) 5 times, k. 1. **20th row**—Purl.

21st row—S. 1, (k. 2, m. 1, k. 2, k. 2 tog.) 5 times, k. 3, inc., inc., k. 3, (k. 2, m. 1, k. 2, k. 2 tog.) 5 times, k. 1.

22nd row—Purl. **23rd row**—S. 1, (k. 3, m. 1, k. 3 tog., m. 1) 6 times, k. 4, (k. 3, m. 1, k. 3 tog., m. 1) 5 times, k. 1. **24th row**—K. 35, inc., inc., k. 35.

25th row—As 7th pattern row.

26th row—Purl. Rep. rows 9-26 inclusive only rep. brackets one more time than stated in each case (86 sts.).

45th row—Cast off 6, s. 1, * k. 1, m. 1, k. 2, k. 2 tog., k. 1, rep. from * till 1 st. remains, k. 1. **46th row**—Cast off 6, p. to end of row. **47th row**—Cast off 6, s. 1, k. 2, * m. 1, k. 3 tog., m. 1, k. 3, rep. from * till 5 sts. remain, m. 1, k. 3 tog., m. 1, k. 2. **48th row**—As 46th row.

49th row—Cast off 6, s. 1, k. 2, * k. 2 tog., k. 1, m. 1, k. 3, rep. from * till 5 sts. remain, k. 2 tog., k. 1, m. 1, k. 2.

50th row—As 46th row. Cast off remaining 50 sts.

Right Back

Cast on 38 sts. on No. 10 needles and work exactly as for Front until 1st row of armhole shaping has been completed

THIS charming model in lace-stitch has such a pretty line at the back, with its crochet buttons and graceful sash-bow.

KNITTING

Short-sleeved Fair Isle sweater

Measurements Bust: 81 [86] cm
(32 [34] in). Length: 48 [50] cm (19½ [20] in)
Materials 7 × 25 gm balls of 4-ply yarn
main colour (N), 2 balls each in W and C
and 1 ball each in B and Y
Needles A pair each of 3-mm (No. 11)
and 4- [4½-] mm (No. 8 [No. 7])
Abbreviations See page 16
Tension 13 sts equal 5 cm (2 in) over
Fair Isle pattern on 4-mm needles

Back

With 3-mm needles and main colour (N)
cast on 106 sts and work in single rib for
9 cm (3½ in) inc. 1 st at each end of last
row (108) sts. Change to 4- [4½-] mm
needles and work in stocking st with the
following colours: **1st and 2nd rows:** W.
3rd to 6th rows: N. **7th and 8th rows:**
W. **9th to 12th rows:** B. **13th and 14th
rows:** W. **15th to 18th rows:** N. **19th
row:** *k1N, k3W rep. from * to end. **20th
row:** p1N, * p1W, p3N rep. from *to last
2 sts, p1W, p1N. **21st and 22nd rows:**
work in N. **23rd row:** work k1N, k1Y all
along row. **24th row:** work purl row in N.
25th row: *k3N, k1Y rep. from * to end.
26th to 28th rows: work in N, inc. 1 st at
end of last row. **29th row:** *k1C, k1N,
k1C, k6N, k1C, k6N, k1C, k1N rep. from
* to last st, k1C. **30th row:** *p2C, p1N,
p1C, p4N, p3C, p4N, p1C, p1N, p1C rep.
from * to last st, p1C. **31st row:** *k1C,
k3N, k1C, k2N, k2C, k1N, k2C, k2N,
k1C, k3N rep. from * to last st, k1C.
32nd row: *p1C, p4N, p1C, p1N, p5C,
p1N, p1C, p4N, rep. from * to last st,

p1C. **33rd row:** *k1N, k1C, k4N, k3C,
k1N, k3C, k4N, k1C rep. from * to last st,
k1N. **34th row:** *p1B, p3N, p3B, p2N,
p1B, p2N, p3B, p3N rep. from * to last
st, p1B. **35th row:** *k3N, k4B, (k1N, k1B)
twice, k1N, k4B, k2N rep. from * to last
st, k1N. **36th row:** *p2N, p2B, (p1N,
p1B) 5 times, p1N, p2B, p1N rep. from *
to last st, p1N. Repeat rows 35 to 29
inclusive. **44th to 46th rows:** work in N.
47th row: *k1Y, k3N rep. from * to last
st, k1Y. **48th row:** p2N, *p1Y, p3N rep.
from * to last 3 sts, p1Y, p2N. **49th and
50th rows:** work in N. **51st row:** work
same as 47th row. **52nd row:** p2W, *p1N,
p3W rep. from * to last 3 sts, p1N, p2W.
53rd row: work same as 47th row. **54th
to 56th rows:** work in N.
At this stage you have reached the
armholes. **Shape armholes:** (*being very
careful to keep the Fair Isle pattern correct*)
by casting off 4 sts at beg. of next 6 rows
and then continue straight until armhole
measures 17 cm (6½ in) from start.
Continue in main colour only. **Shape
shoulders:** by casting off 9 sts at beg. of
each of next 6 rows, inc. 1 st at end
of last row. Then change to 3-mm needles
and in main colour work in single rib for
2½ cm (1 in). **Cast off** *ribwise*.

Front

Work exactly as for back until armhole
measures 10 cm (4 in). **Shape the
neck:** work across 35 sts, slip next 29 sts
on to a spare safety-pin, work to end of
row. Continue on latter set of sts, dec. 1 st

at neck edge on *every* row until 27 sts remain. Continue straight until front armhole measures same as that of the back. Break off colours and continue in main colour only. **Shape shoulder:** cast off 9 sts at beg. of each of next 3 rows which start at armhole edge. Rejoin yarn to centre edge of remaining sts and work to correspond, reversing shapings. Change to 3-mm needles and with main colour only and right side of work facing pick up 25 sts from left front of neck, work across 29 sts on spare safety-pin, pick up 26 sts up right front neck and work 2½ cm (1 in) in single rib. **Cast off** *ribwise*.

Sleeves (2)

Using 3-mm needles and main colour cast on 72 sts and work in single rib for 3 cm (1¼ in). Change to 4- [4½-] mm needles and work in Fair Isle pattern from row 29 to row 56 inclusive, inc. 1 st at each end of the 5th and every following 4th row until there are 90 sts on needle. Continue straight to row 56 of Fair Isle pattern.

Shape top: (*being very careful to keep the Fair Isle pattern correct throughout the rest of the sleeve*) cast off 4 sts at beg. of next 6 rows. Then continue straight for 10 cm (4 in). Now cast off 4 sts at beg. of *every* row until 18 sts remain. **Cast off.**

Making up

Sew shoulder seams of back and front together and sew sleeves into armholes gathering all surplus fullness to the top. If yarn appropriate, press work lightly (see the note on page 16) omitting ribbing. Sew side and sleeve seams.

Some suggested colour combinations

main colour:	grey or	navy or	white or	camel
1st contrast:	rust	grey	red	cream
2nd contrast:	cream	rust	navy	chocolate
3rd contrast:	burgundy	cream	pale blue	airforce blue (greyish blue)
4th contrast:	yellow	mid blue	yellow	rust
main colour:	pale blue	black	red	moss green
1st contrast:	burgundy	camel	turquoise	dark green
2nd contrast:	white	cream	navy·	cream
3rd contrast:	red	gold	grey	dull gold
4th contrast:	emerald	rust	yellow	mid blue

Man's moss stitch and rib waistcoat

Measurements (allowing for certain stretch of ribbed back so waistcoat fits snugly) 91 [97, 102] cm (36 [38, 40] in)
Materials 13 [13, 14] × 25 gm balls of double-knitting yarn and 6 buttons
Needles A pair each of 3½-mm (No. 9) and 4½-mm (No. 7)
Abbreviations See page 16
Tension 11 sts equal 5 cm (2 in) in Moss st using 4½-mm (No. 7) needles

Back
Using 3½-mm (No. 9) needles cast on 95 [101, 107] sts and work in single rib for 8 cm (3 in), inc. 1 st at each end of last row. Change to 4½-mm (No. 7) needles and continue to work in single rib, inc. 1 st at each end of every 10th row until there are 105 [111, 117] sts on needle. Work straight until back measures 31 cm (12 in) from start. Begin to work in armhole garter st band. **Next row:** sl1, k6 rib to last 7 sts, k6, k1 tbl. Continue like this with 7 sts garter st band until this band is 22 [22, 23] cm (8½ [8¾, 9] in) ending front facing. **Shape shoulder:** by casting off 12 sts at beginning of next row and 10 sts at beginning of following 2 alt. rows. Work 6 rows in garter st. **Cast off** remaining sts.

Right front
Using 4½-mm needles (No. 7) cast on 38 sts and work in garter st for 6 rows. Start front shaping as follows: **1st row:** k5, m1 (by k1, p1 into next st) moss st 6, turn. **2nd row:** and every alt. row. Moss st to last 5 sts, k5. **3rd row:** k5, m1, moss st 12, turn.

5th row: k5, m1, moss st 18, turn. **7th row:** k5, m1, moss st 24, turn. **9th row:** k5, m1, moss st to end. **10th row:** as row 2. Repeat rows 9 and 10 until there are 50 [52, 54] sts on needle. Continue in moss st with the 5 sts garter st border at the front edge, until work measures 11 cm (4½ in) at the *side* edge, finishing at *front* edge.

Buttonhole row: k2 wl.fwd k2 tog. k1, moss st to end. Work 13 rows in moss st with garter st front border. Repeat these 14 rows until side edge measures 31 cm (12 in) (same as back), finishing at side edge. **Next row:** sl1, k6 moss st to last 5 sts, k5. **Next row:** k5, k2 tog., tbl moss st to last 7, k7. **Next row:** k7, moss st to last 5 sts, k5. **Next row:** k5, moss st to last 7, k7. Repeat last 4 rows until 32 sts remain. Then continue straight until armhole garter st border measures same as back, ending at side edge. **Shape shoulder:** by casting off 12 sts at beg. of next row and 10 sts at beg. of following 2 alt. rows.

Left front
Work as for right front, reversing all shapings and omitting buttonholes.

Pockets (2)
Using 4½-mm (No. 7) needles cast on 26 sts and work in moss st for 11 cm (4½ in). **Cast off** in moss st.

Making up
Sew pockets just above point shaping at centre of each side. Sew up shoulder and side seams. Attach buttons.

KNITTING

Feather stitch waistcoat

Measurements The feather stitch pattern is loose and 'gives', so this one size fits most people from bust size 81–91 cm (32–36 in)
Materials 8 × 25 gm balls of double-knitting yarn or mohair
Needles A pair each of 4½-mm (No. 7) and 6½-mm (No. 3)
Abbreviations See page 16

Note
Always slip first stitch and knit into back of last stitch on every row while knitting this garment as this gives neat and tidy edges.

Back and both fronts (all one piece to armhole). It will be necessary for you to make a buttonhole on the 5th row, and on every following 12th row till 6 have been worked. To make a buttonhole sl1, k2, wl.fwd, k2 tog., k1 (on the border). Using 4½-mm needles cast on 131 sts and work 10 cm (4 in) in single rib. Change to 6½-mm needles and pattern as follows: 1st row: knit. 2nd row: k6, p to last 6 sts, k6. 3rd row: k6 *p2 tog., k1 (wl. fwd, k1) twice, p2 tog., rep. from * to last 6 sts, k6. 4th row: k6, p to last 6 sts, k6. 5th row: knit. 6th row: k6 *k2 tog., p1 (wrn, p1) twice, k2 tog., rep. from * to last 6 sts, k6. These 6 rows form the pattern. Continue in pattern until work is 36 cm (14 in), *keeping the pattern correct* as follows: 1st row: knit. 2nd row: k6, p14, k28, p35, k28, p14, k6. 3rd row: k6, pattern 14, k28, pattern 35, k28, pattern 14, k6. 4th row: as 2nd. 5th row: knit. 6th row: k6, pattern 14, k7, cast off 14, k7, pattern 35, k7, cast off 14, k7, pattern 14, k6. Continue on 1st group of sts keeping k6 front border and k7 arm border on every row. Work 6 complete patterns (36 rows). **Cast off** *knitwise*. Return to centre group of stitches for back, keeping a k7 border at both ends of every row. Work to same length as front. **Cast off** *knitwise*. Work other front to match 1st front until 6 patterns have been worked and then cast off sleeve border sts and 14 pattern sts, leaving the 7 front border sts. Continue to work on these sts in garter st for about 8 cm (3 in) to go across centre back of neck. **Cast off** *knitwise*.

Making up
Sew borders together at cast-off edges and then to back neck.

KNITTING

4-ply cardigan with Fair Isle yoke

Measurements Bust 84 [89] cm (33[35]in). Length: 50[51]cm(19½[20]in). Sleeve seam: 47 cm (18 in)

Materials 10 × 25 gm balls 4-ply yarn, oddments in 5 colours and 12 buttons to match.

Needles A pair each of 2½-mm (No. 12) and 3½-mm (No. 9)

Abbreviations See page 16

Tension 13 sts equal 5 cm (2 in) on 3½-mm needles

Fair Isle Colour Code
N: natural (main colour)
B: blue
G: green
R: red
Y: yellow
Br: brown

Back
Using 2½-mm needles and main colour cast on 100 [112] sts and work in single rib for 34 rows. Change to 3½-mm needles and work in stocking st for 34 rows. Inc. 1 st at each end of the next and every following 4th row until there are 110 [122] sts on needle, after which continue straight until work measures 32 [33] cm (12½ [13] in). **Shape armholes:** by casting off 10 sts at beg. of each of next 2 rows, then dec. 1 st at the beg. only of the next 5 [5] rows (85 [97]) sts. Work 20 more rows in stocking st ending with wrong side facing. Then work 25 rows of Fair Isle as follows: **1st row:** (*wrong side*) p1G *p1N, p3G, p1N, p1G, rep. from * to end. **2nd row:** k in N. **3rd row:** p1N, *p2B, p2N, rep. from * to end. **4th row:** as 3rd (k row).

5th row: *p2R, p2N, rep. from * to last st, p1R. **6th row:** k as 5th. **7th row:** p in N. **8th row:** k1G, *k1N, k3G, k1N, k1G, rep. from * to end. **9th row:** p in N. **10th row:** kBr, *k2N, k1Br, k1N, k3Br, k1N, k1Br, k2N, k1Br, rep. from * to end. **11th row:** p1N, *p1Br, p3N, p3Br, p3N, p1Br, p1N, rep. from * to end. **12th row:** k1Y, *k1Br, k1Y, k2Br, k1Y, k1Br, k1Y, k2Br, k1Y, k1Br, k1Y, rep. from * to end. **13th row:** p1Br, *p2Y, p3Br, p1Y, p3Br, p2Y, k1Br, rep. from * to end. Now work from 12th row back to 1st row inclusive – but knit instead of purl and vice versa (pattern of 25 rows). **Shape shoulders:** in main colour cast off 9 [10] sts at beg. of next 6 rows. Leave remaining sts on a spare needle to pick up for neckband.

Right front
In main colour cast on 60 [66] sts and work 2 rows of single rib. **3rd row:** rib 2, cast off 3 sts, work in single rib to end. **4th row:** work in single rib casting on 3 sts over those cast off to finish buttonhole. Work 8 rows in single rib. Rep. last 10 rows twice more then work another buttonhole on next 2 rows, which completes 34 rows of rib as on back. Change to 3½-mm needles. **Next row:** (k1, p1) 5 times for single rib band (which is continued to neckline) k to end. **Next row:** p to last 10 sts, rib 10. Rep. last 2 rows 4 times more, then work 2 rows with a buttonhole. Rep. last 12 rows twice more then inc. 1 st at side edge of next row. Work 3 rows straight. Make 4 more

94

incs. at side edge in this way at the same time working buttonholes as before on every 11th and 12th row. There should now be 65 [71] sts on needle. Continue straight till work measures same as back up to armhole finishing at side edge. **Shape armhole:** by casting off 10 sts at beg. of next row, work to last 10 sts, rib 10. Work 5 more rows dec. 1 st at armhole edge on each row. Work 20 rows straight finishing with wrong side facing. Work across 1st row of Fair Isle pattern to last 17 sts. Turn, leaving these last 17 sts on a spare needle or pin to pick up for neckband. Now continue with 25 rows of Fair Isle pattern, as on back, dec. 1 st at neck end of every alt. row 6 [9] times. Then continue straight until Fair Isle pattern is complete. Work back in main colour to armhole edge. **Shape shoulder:** by casting off 9 [10] sts at beg. of next and following 2 alt. rows.

Left front
Work as for right front, reversing all shapings and omitting buttonholes.

Sleeves (2)
In main colour and using 2½-mm needles cast on 50 sts and work in single rib for 9 cm (3½ in), then last row as follows: work 20 sts, k twice into each of the next 10 sts, work 20 sts (60 sts). Change to 3½-mm needles and work stocking st for 44 rows. Then inc. 1 st at each end of the next and every following 4th row until there are 78 sts on needle. Continue straight till sleeve measures 47 cm (18½ in) from beg. **Shape sleeve top:** cast off 12 sts at beg. of next 2 rows then work 28 rows dec. 1 st at each end of every alt. row (60 sts). Then k3 tog. all along next row (20 sts). Purl 1 row. **Cast off.**

Neckband
Sew up shoulder seams. Then with right side of work facing and using 2½-mm needles, starting with the right front neck pick up 17 sts left at centre front, 26 sts up side of front, 34 [37] sts from back, 26 sts down other front and 17 sts from left centre front. Work 8 rows in single rib making a buttonhole as before on 6th and 7th rows. **Cast off** ribwise.

Making up
If yarn is suitable, carefully press all pieces on wrong side with a damp cloth, avoiding ribbing. Set sleeves into armholes, arranging any extra fullness at top. Sew sleeve and side seams in one line. Press any seams if necessary and sew buttons on left front to correspond with buttonholes.

The car that made 14 *h.p.* motoring famous

THE history of 14 h.p. motoring since 1933 is really the history of the Vauxhall Fourteen. Before the introduction of Vauxhall the sale of *all* 14 h.p. cars had averaged only 10,000 a year. In five years this has been almost trebled and nearly 100,000 owners are now enjoying 14 h.p. motoring at the wheel of a Vauxhall.

This success has inspired our engineers to build the new, bigger, Luxury Fourteen for 1939. Since the Motor Show the demand for this new car has taxed even Vauxhall's manufacturing resources. Only by trebling our original manufacturing schedules are we beginning to catch up with the demand—and reasonably early delivery can now be given.

The New VAUXHALL "14" SIX

Before you decide on your next car, see and try the new Fourteen at your local Vauxhall dealers'. Write for literature to Vauxhall Motors Ltd., Luton, Beds.

NOTICE *the clean rear lines and the big luggage boot. The spare wheel is housed in a separate compartment.*

THE NEW VAUXHALL FOURTEEN IS

BIGGER
with longer wheelbase, wider track, and much more roomy coachwork,

LIVELIER
the new 6-cylinder engine gives more and *smoother* power,

SAFER
all-steel integral construction and hydraulic brakes,

EASIER TO DRIVE
all silent all synchromesh gears, adjustable steering wheel, etc., etc.,

SMOOTHER
latest Vauxhall torsion bar, Independent Springing, trouble free, steady on corners,

MORE LUXURIOUS
arm rests to all seats and many new luxury features,

AND ECONOMICAL
30 miles per gallon at an average speed of 30 m.p.h.

DE LUXE SALOON

£230

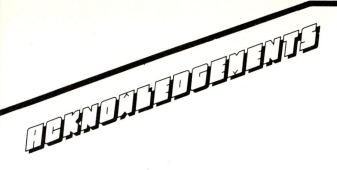

ACKNOWLEDGEMENTS

The author and publishers would like to thank
the National Portrait Gallery for
supplying the prints used on
pages 6, 36, 43, 47, 63, 83 and 97,
and the Radio Times Hulton
Picture Library for permission to
reproduce the pictures of Coco Chanel
and Lady Abdy and of the Duke of
Windsor which appear on pages 11, 30-31,
60–61 and 90–91, together with the
photographs on pages 102–103